W9-CBD-287

TO ART GILKEY

K2

The Savage Mountain

by Charles S. Houston, M.D.
Robert H. Bates

and Members of the Third American Karakoram Expedition
Colonel M. Ata-Ullah
Robert H. Bates
George I. Bell
Robert W. Craig
Arthur K. Gilkey
Charles S. Houston
Dee Molenaar
Peter Schoening
Capt. H.R.A. Streather

K2
The Savage Mountain

THE ADVENTURE LIBRARY

The text of this edition of *K2* has been computer typeset in
Adobe Garamond, designed by Robert Slimbach after original
typefaces created by Claude Garamond of Antwerp, Belgium,
in the16th century.

*Typography and binding design for The Adventure Library by
Elton S. Robinson.*

*Production management by Martin Cook Associates, Ltd., New York
Printing and binding by Braun-Brumfield, Inc.*

Copyright © 1954, 1979, 1994 by Charles S. Houston
and Robert H. Bates

Foreword Copyright © 1994 by The Adventure Library
Maps and drawings © Dee Molenaar
Endpaper map drawing by Richard L. Burdsall

The photographs in this book were taken by members of the
Third American Karakoram Expedition and are reproduced
by arrangement with them.

New sketches and maps have enhanced this edition of *K2* through
the courtesy of expedition member Dee Molenaar, who is currently
preparing an autobiographical work that includes his mountain art.

All rights reserved. No part of this book may be reproduced in any
manner whatsoever without written permission from the publisher
except in the case of brief quotations embodied in critical articles
and reviews.

First Adventure Library Edition 1994

The Adventure Library
79 Nash Road
Purdys, New York 10578

Library of Congress Catalog Number: 94-072543
ISBN: 1-885283-01-6

Printed in the United States of America

Something from those storm-swept days has been fused into our bones and will never leave us. It has made a brotherhood, a special kind of friendship that is very rare and very precious.

Robert H. Bates

Contents

Illustrations

Preface

Himalayan mountaineering is a type of exploration which must be conducted within very exacting limitations, both physical and human. They are so exacting that there is little margin for error or bad luck. With the best of planning and expedition management they make the chances for success so slim that only a very fortunate combination of events can bring the summit within reach. It is not surprising, therefore, that many years of determined efforts by strong parties can go by with a major summit still unattained.

Only rarely have the Himalayan giants been overcome on the first major attempt. Generally they have resisted attacks through several generations of climbers and have required a slow, painful build-up of information and experience over many years of effort. This gradually produces a clearer picture of the obstacles that must be overcome, and at the same time skills and techniques to cope with them are developed and perfected. Finally the stage is set, the right combination of party, mountain conditions, weather, and luck comes together—and the mountain is climbed.

The importance of the achievement is primarily in the skill, judgment, and courage of the team. Beyond that, however, and of even more lasting significance, is the fact that the final success is built on the past efforts of many others—often of different nationalities and races. They have known the bitter disappointment of defeat, tempered only slightly by the realization that they had exerted their best efforts. Only when the mountain is climbed can their struggles be seen in true perspective as positive, hard-won steps toward a common goal. Then the pioneers can justly share in the victor's accomplishment and be truly happy that their summit has at last been reached.

My thoughts were hardly so objective as my friends and I retreated from the upper slopes of K2 on the First American Karakoram Expedition in 1938. We realized that the summit was not to be ours and that problems of supply and approaching bad weather demanded immediate descent.

It softened our disappointment to know that we had unlocked some of the mountain's major secrets, and that a practical route had been established to within striking distance of the summit. We thought we had a clear picture of the mountain, and there was little doubt in our minds that another strong party—perhaps including some of us—given reasonable luck with weather, would make the summit.

However, in 1938 we were never able fully to assess the weather hazard, although we had plenty of respect for it, or to comprehend clearly the problems of evacuating a sick or injured member of the party from high on the mountain, let alone a combination of both. The experience of the next two expeditions showed that the picture was fainter than we thought and that we had only partially understood the mountain's defenses. The 1953 expedition, whose heroic story is told in this book, brought the picture into sharper focus. Its members brought back a truer picture of weather problems which will be invaluable to future expeditions to K2. More important, they demonstrated that a strong, well-organized, and well-equipped party could survive prolonged exposure to severe weather and still retreat in good order over an extremely difficult route.

Though defeated in its attempt, the 1953 expedition's success in overcoming almost impossible problems of survival will continue to give strength and encouragement to mountaineers in peril on the high peaks.

William P. House

Foreword

For many climbers, K2—even more than Everest—is the ultimate mountain. At 28,250 feet, it is second only to Everest by a scant 800 feet. With its classic pyramidal shape, K2 is steep on all sides. It is the perfect embodiment of our mental image of what a great mountain should be. The climber who has designs on K2's summit must contend not only with extreme altitude and difficult rock and ice, but with sudden storms that deplete strength and erode will power. Nearly a hundred climbers have now reached K2's summit, but thirty-three of those attempting the mountain have died in the process. Its reputation as both the most difficult and the most dangerous of the world's fourteen 8,000-meter peaks is well deserved.

In the history of Himalayan mountaineering, the 1953 American expedition to K2 stands out as one of the most memorable. *K2: The Savage Mountain,* by Charles Houston, Robert Bates, and other members of the Third American Karakoram Expedition, now reissued in The Adventure Library series, chronicles their valiant attempt to make the first ascent of K2 after two other American expeditions nearly succeeded in 1938 and 1939. The account of their climb is as riveting today as it was forty years ago.

Displaying an abundance of courage, tenacity, and strength in the face of almost overwhelming odds against their safe return, the Charles Houston–led team survived a severe ten-day storm at 25,000 feet on K2 and an accident that almost ended in disaster when virtually the entire team was involved in a fall down the mountain's exposed upper slopes. Only Peter Schoening's now legendary ice ax belay saved his teammates from certain death.

This happened in the midst of their heroic effort to evacuate Art Gilkey from the highest camp. Stricken with blood clots in his leg, Gilkey could not descend without assistance from the others. After the accident, the sick man was lashed to the slope while the climbers injured in the fall were assisted to a nearby campsite. When they returned for Gilkey ten minutes later, to their shock and disbelief he had been swept into the abyss. Gilkey's death most likely was due to avalanche. But it is not beyond the realm of possibility that Gilkey sacrificed himself to save the others. The answer will never be known. It took the survivors five more storm-filled days to reach the safety of base camp.

Hillary and Tenzing's climb to the top of Everest earlier that same summer provided the world with electrifying news. But the events on K2 are the stuff of legends and are even more striking with the passage of time. The climbers' struggle with wind, storm, sickness, high altitude, and the loss of their companion seems more poignant than the efforts of other expeditions that achieved success. Why is this so? Oddly, it has to do with the fact that they did not succeed. When a mountain is climbed for the first time—particularly if it is an Everest or a K2—there is a great deal of fanfare that attends success. But when the effort falls short of the goal and the climbers are faced with a situation that threatens their lives, the story is more compelling—especially when a tragic dimension is present, as it was on K2 in 1953.

The most remarkable aspect of the 1953 expedition was the way these men stayed together—through thick and thin—to the end. There was absolutely no thought of leaving Gilkey to save themselves. They would get down together or not at all. In the years that followed—most notably during that tragic summer of 1986, when thirteen climbers lost their lives—equally dramatic events have occurred on K2. But never has the 1953 expedition's unified resolve in the face of extreme peril been matched. It was what enabled these men to survive one of the epic experiences of Himalayan mountaineering. It was what enabled them to maintain lifelong friendships afterward.

The 1953 expedition, like its forerunners in 1938 and 1939, was carried off in the finest style. Lightweight in comparison with other Himalayan expeditions of the same period, these early American attempts on K2 came very close to success. K2 was finally climbed in 1954, but by a much larger expedition. An Italian team under the leadership of Professor Ardito Desio, who had explored the area around K2 in 1929 with the Duke of Spoleto, came not merely to climb K2, but, in the leader's word, "to conquer the mountain." Taking the same route—the Abruzzi Ridge—that the three previous American expeditions had established, Achille Compagnoni and Lino Lacedelli walked onto the summit at 6:00 P.M. on July 31, oxygen-starved from having their bottles run out a few hundred feet below.

The ascent of K2 was not repeated for another twenty-four years. In 1977 a massive team of fifty Japanese climbers followed the route of its predecessors, with seven team members, including a Pakistani, eventually reaching the summit. The following year, a fourteen-member team led by Jim Whittaker became the fifth American expedition to tackle K2. (Two others—in 1960 and 1975—came nowhere near the summit.) Four of us who participated in the 1978 expedition, including Whittaker, were veterans of the 1975 American attempt of K2's Northwest Ridge. On that climb, a double-corniced, knife-edge ridge had stopped us cold at 22,000 feet on top of the first of a series of sharp, ice-festooned pinnacles.

In 1978 we wanted to attempt K2 via its difficult Northeast Ridge, a route that had defeated a strong Polish team two years before. Deep snow and avalanche conditions, however, prevented our team from achieving this goal. Instead, from the Polish route at the base of the summit pyramid we made an exposed traverse beneath a huge, threatening icecliff to link up with the route the Italians had taken in 1954.

Near the intersection of the two routes, we were able to pitch our small tent at 25,800 feet on the downhill side of a crevasse that offered minimal protection from the icecliff overhead. From there, Lou Reichardt and I climbed to the summit on September 6, 1978. John Roskelley and Rick Ridgeway, who had retreated from their attempt to complete the avalanche-threatened Polish route to the summit, retraced our steps across the dangerous traverse and repeated our summit climb a day later.

In the fading light of late afternoon as we neared the summit, I recall being filled with a tremendous sense of history and admiration for what had gone on so many years before. I could look down to where Houston's team had withstood the week-long storm. The site of the accident was clearly visible. I could also see the crest of the famed Abruzzi Ridge, which dropped off steeply to the Godwin-Austen Glacier more than 12,000 feet below us.

As Reichardt and I walked those last few steps to the summit, I could feel the presence of Houston, Bates, Schoening, and the others who, but for the vagaries of storm and circumstance, would have been there a quarter-century ahead of us. Their struggle and character is one of the great stories of modern mountaineering.

Jim Wickwire
Seattle, 1994

The Call to Climb

During the terrible days of storm at Camp VIII we thought seldom of the reasons which had brought us to the mountain; all our energy was focused on survival. We were trapped in three small mountain tents near the summit of the highest unclimbed mountain on earth, trapped by an endless storm of wind and snow which made impossible advance or retreat. All eight of us had been working for two months to establish this high camp and another one still higher from which two men might reach the top. All eight of us and many others had been planning for a year to make the expedition possible. During the ten days of hardship and disappointment, of pain and tragedy, which climaxed our venture, we spoke of the summit and of home, we remembered other storms and other critical times. No one tried to answer the question then, "Why? Why climb mountains?"

In the years that have passed since our ordeal we have been asked that question many times and have answered it in many ways. No answer is complete or satisfactory. Perhaps there is no single answer; perhaps each climber must have his own reasons for such an effort. The answer cannot be simple; it is compounded of such elements as the great beauty of clear cold air, of colors beyond the ordinary, of the lure of unknown regions beyond the rim of experience. The pleasure of physical fitness, the pride of conquering a steep and difficult rock pitch, the thrill of danger—but danger controlled by skill—are also there. How can I phrase what seems to me the most important reason of all? It is the chance to be briefly free of the small concerns of our common lives, to strip off nonessentials, to come down to the core of life itself. Food, shelter, friends—these are the essentials, these plus faith and purpose and a deep and unrelenting determination. On great mountains all purpose is concentrated on the single job at hand, yet the summit is but a token of success, and the attempt is worthy in itself. It is for these reasons that we climb, and in climbing find something greater than accomplishment.

This is the story of an expedition that failed to reach its summit. It is the story of a venture made for sport and not for gain, of a small, compact expedition rather than a large and organized campaign. But more than that, it is the story of a team of men from three nations, a team that tried and tried again, that faced privation and danger, that suffered much but gained more. In a tiny way ours is the story of other ventures, bigger, older, braver, but ventures which have made and will make man great. As Maurice Herzog said, speaking of his ordeal on another great Himalayan peak, "There are other Annapurnas in the lives of men."

Charles S. Houston

K2

The Savage Mountain

1 *Historical and Geographical*

ROBERT H. BATES

In Central Asia, 5 miles higher than all the oceans, thousands of tons of ice and snow hang from the precipitous south side of K2, the second highest mountain in the world. Here for a few days in the summer of 1939 a tiny tent with one American in it clung to a small shelf of snow, which projected out above thousands of feet of empty space. In this tent, remote from civilization, lay Dudley Wolfe of Boston, cut off completely from his closest companions, who were thousands of feet below him. Then, on July 28, 1939, two Sherpa porters, Pasang Kikuli and Tsering, made one of the most amazing climbs in mountaineering history. In one day they ascended nearly 7,000 feet of dangerous rock and snow to reach Camp VI at 23,300 feet on K2. On the way they were joined by two other Sherpas, who had previously climbed to Camp IV. These four men spent that night on a narrow ledge of rock 1,500 feet below the snow shelf where Dudley Wolfe lay trapped in his tent without communication with those below. He could not descend alone. His rescuers had food and fuel for only two days. They were risking their own necks in going so high with such a slender food supply, but another man's life was at stake.

Next day three of the Sherpas climbed up a dangerous gully above Camp VI and across steps previously cut in a great ice slope that drops off 7,000 feet in one precipitous swoop to the base of K2. Beyond, on relatively flat snow, they found Dudley

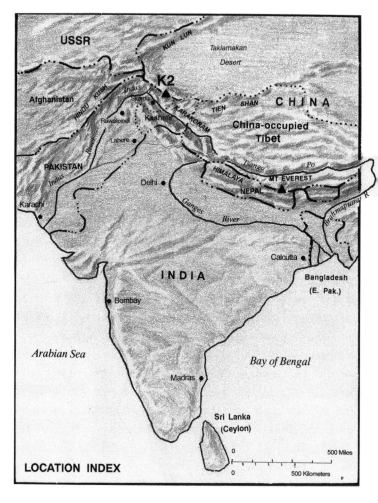

Wolfe. Exposure to altitude had weakened him, so that when the Sherpas reached his tent he was almost too feeble to stand. He was too weak to climb down the mountain but too heavy for the porters to carry. The Sherpas cooked him a meal and explained that they had little food at the camp below but would come back for him. The next day, when they climbed up to him again across the dangerous slabs, he was to come with them or give them a note saying that he was done for, too far gone to make the descent. The weather, they told him, would almost certainly prevent any further rescue attempt.

Weather was stormy next morning, but on July 31, the same three Sherpas said good-by to Tsering at Camp VI and set out on their last trip to Camp VII, where Dudley Wolfe was awaiting them. They were never seen again! Nor has any trace been found of the brave man they sought to rescue.

From that month until June, 1953, nobody set foot on K2, although the challenge of this stupendous mountain was not diminished by the tragedy. Instead, the mystery of what had happened to the four men of the Second American Karakoram Expedition in 1939 increased the challenge of the mountain; for K2 has long been a lodestone pulling men to the little-known magnificence of the Karakoram Range, and to the "mountaineer's mountain." Few people, however, know the geographic position or history of exploration of this remote area.

Among the great mountain ranges of the world, none is so famous for giant peaks and untrodden passes as the mighty Himalayas, which for 1,500 miles separate the dry plateaus of Central Asia from the moist and fertile regions to the south. But the Himalayas do not form the continental divide. Instead, the height of land is formed by lower ranges, even more remote from centers of population, that run east and west across Tibet and join to the west with the jagged backbone of the Karakoram Range.

The Karakoram, a massif of wild, forbidding peaks, is located north and slightly west of the Himalayas, and extends for 300 miles from the Shyok River to the Hindu Kush Range. Within this 300-mile sweep, one-fifth the extent of the Himalayas, the Karakoram has the longest high rampart in the world, a continuous crest of high peaks 104 miles long. The Karakoram has thirty-three peaks over 24,000 feet compared to the forty-two in the entire system of the Himalayas, while within 18 miles of K2 eight peaks rise to over 25,000 feet, and others of equal height are not far away. The Karakoram Range consists of several smaller groups, called *muztaghs* (*muz* meaning ice and *tagh* mountain), the highest of which, the Baltoro Muztagh, forms the continental divide and has as its dominant point 28,250-

foot K2. Probably nowhere else in the world do so many giant peaks rise from so small an area as in the Baltoro Muztagh.

The name Karakoram, which means black rock, sometimes deceives people, for it was also the name of a prosperous city in Chinese Turkestan north of the mountains. This was the Mongol capital under the great emperor Genghiz Khan, but after Kublai Khan moved the capital to Peking in 1267, this great city began to decline and eventually was so completely swallowed up by the desert that its remains were not rediscovered until 1889. Although the Karakoram Pass, some 75 miles to the east of K2, is still used, and the Karakoram Range is known to mountain climbers across the world, the man-made city of Karakoram has disappeared beneath the sands of Central Asia.

The name K2 was one of a number of provisional designations given by the Survey of India. K stood for Karakoram, and the peaks of the area were numbered in rough order. K1 was later called Masherbrum, and K3, K4, and K5 became known officially as the Gasherbrum peaks. To add to the confusion, at one time it was decided to renumber the peaks to produce continuity from west to east, and accordingly in some early publications K2 *was renamed K13!* The symbol K2 had already become widely known around the world, however, and this confusing duplication of symbols was quickly eliminated and K2 became again K2. That is still its official name.

To complicate matters still further, however, K2 on many maps is called Godwin-Austen, for Maj. Gen. H. H. Godwin-Austen, a well-known English geographer and surveyor of the mid-nineteenth century on whose tombstone are carved the words "He surveyed the Karakoram." Explorers and topographers have tried to discover an established native name for the giant rock and ice mountain. Although Chogori, Lamba Pahar, Dapsang, and Lanfafahad have been mentioned, today natives in adjacent areas appear most likely to call it Kechu (K2) or Cheku or even Kechu Kangri (K2 Ice Mountain).

The exact altitude of K2 was also a source of controversy for a number of years, but as the Survey of India has pointed out,

Aerial View
K2 FROM SOUTHWEST

© D. MOLENAAR 1979

the height of K2 has probably been measured as accurately as the height of any of the world's highest mountains. The height first given by the survey was 28,278 feet, but "the value now accepted is 28,250 feet." Mount Everest is officially listed as being 752 feet higher and Kangchenjunga 104 feet lower; but such accurate judgments are of course impossible.

Everest and the other great Nepalese peaks rise about 900 miles to the east of K2. Between these giants stretch Buddhist Ladakh and Tibet, while north and northwest lie the uncharted wastes of Sinkiang (Chinese Turkestan) and Russian Turkestan and, even farther to the west, Afghanistan. K2 obviously has a fascinating geographical position. Almost exactly on the opposite side of the Northern Hemisphere from Denver, Colorado, K2 has approximately the same latitude as North Carolina and Tokyo. China owns the land to the north and east, the side seen by Younghusband in 1887 and later by Shipton and Tilman of the Shaksgam Expedition in 1939, but they made no careful examination of the precipitous north wall. The other thirty-three expeditions to visit the Karakoram apparently never saw this side.

The first European to see K2 was probably the surveyor Montgomerie in 1858, but Godwin-Austen and others of Montgomerie's party apparently saw it while surveying the lower Baltoro Glacier in 1861. This group did not get to the base of K2, nor did Sir Martin Conway, who in 1892 explored the Baltoro Glacier to Concordia. Just as Conway profited by the experience of his predecessors in the Karakoram, so Eckenstein, who had been with Conway, used Conway's map in 1902 when his party explored the Godwin-Austen Glacier and found at its head Windy Gap, then thought to be a possible pass into Chinese Turkestan. This party made the first attempt to climb K2. It consisted of three Englishmen (Eckenstein, Crowley, and Knowles), two Austrians (Drs. Wesseley and Pfannl), and the Swiss Dr. Guillarmod. On July 10, 1902, they attempted to climb to the crest of the long Northeast Ridge, but were turned back about 150 feet below the crest at a height of approximately 21,400 feet. Steep snow with hard ice under it defeated them, but bad weather was also a severe handicap. On July 21, 1902, Eckenstein wrote, "We established our Camp X, height about 18,600 feet, just 49 days ago. Since then we've had 8 partially fine days (no 3 consecutive) and the rest of the time continuous snowstorms. Never anywhere in the world have I experienced such bad weather. Our present snow storm has gone on for over 96 hours, and shows as yet no sign of abatement. At our camp here there are over 5 feet of fresh snow."

On the expedition's return, Guillarmod stated in his book *Six Mois dans l'Himalaya* the belief that K2 could be climbed by the Northeast Ridge. This statement intrigued the famous Italian explorer Prince Luigi Amedeo of Savoy, Duke of the Abruzzi, who in 1909 led the next expedition to K2. With him were Dr. Filippo de Filippi and the renowned photographer Vittorio Sella, as well as seven guides and porters from Courmayeur. The party reached Base Camp below the tremendous south wall of K2 on May 26, and four days later the duke attempted to climb the Southeast Ridge. He established a camp at 18,245 feet, and from there the guides climbed upward 1,000 feet to leave loads on a narrow saddle. Next day the guides returned to the saddle and went on to a height of "certainly 20,000 feet." Here they gave up the climb "not because they had encountered insurmountable obstacles, but because it was hopeless to think of bringing so long and formidable an ascent to a successful issue, when from the very first steps they had met with such difficulties as made the climb barely possible to guides not hampered by loads, and put out of the question the conveying of luggage necessary to keep one from perishing from cold and exhaustion."

Next the duke entered the Savoia Glacier and went up it along the northwest side of K2. Here on June 7, after four hours of climbing, he reached the West Ridge at an elevation of 21,870 feet. Unfortunately the cornice was a big one and blocked the view of the north side of K2, but he could tell that the slope below must drop off very steeply on the far side. "As a reward for his labors," Dr. de Filippi wrote, "the duke thus saw utterly annihilated the hopes with which he had begun the ascent." Three weeks later a view of K2 from Skyang Kangri convinced the duke of the futility of attempting to climb the Northeast Ridge of K2 or indeed of making any other attempt to climb the world's second highest mountain.

This lavish expedition established the reputation of K2 as a mountain that would never be climbed. On the duke's return to Europe Sir Martin Conway's remark was significant of the opinion of the day: "Every foot of a route may be climbable, and yet if it cannot all be climbed in one day and there is nowhere to spend a night, what can you do?"

Such was the opinion of many climbers as late as 1929, when Aimone di Savoia-Aosta, Duke of Spoleto, led another Italian expedition to K2, but for the purpose of cartography only. Spoleto's expedition was scientific, but the next party to reach the upper Baltoro went to secure motion pictures. After a brief examination of Hidden Peak (Gasherbrum I), this group, led by Dr. and Mrs. Dyhrenfurth, a well-known Swiss team, climbed two of the lower mountains to the east: the Golden Throne (23,990 feet) and Queen Mary Peak (24,350 feet).

The upper Baltoro was visited next by the first French expedition to try to climb an 8,000-meter peak. This party, led by Henry de Segogne and consisting of nine carefully selected French mountaineers, took thirty-five Sherpas. The party did not visit K2, but instead made a serious attempt on Hidden Peak (26,470 feet), where they were turned back by bad weather after reaching an altitude of 22,960 feet. Two Sherpas were hurt in a 2,000-foot fall during the expedition and had to be carried 360 miles back to Srinagar. Most remarkable of all perhaps was the fact that this prodigious expedition required *650 porters* to transport it from the last village, Askole, to the foot of Hidden Peak.

Such was the record in the Baltoro Muztagh until 1938, when the American Alpine Club sent out a "reconnaissance party" to examine K2 and scout out if possible a potential route to the summit. Number one objective was to make as thorough an examination of K2 as possible, for though an Italian, a Swiss, and a French expedition had seen K2 since the Duke of the Abruzzi attempted to climb it in 1909, twenty-nine years before, none of these men had set foot on the mountain or returned to the Karakoram to try to climb it. K2's reputation was not inviting.

The First American Karakoram Expedition (1938) was led by Dr. Charles S. Houston, then of New York City, who had been a member of the British-American Himalayan Expedition, which in 1936 had reached the summit of Nanda Devi (25,600 feet) in Garhwal, the highest mountain then climbed. With him was Richard L. Burdsall,* who had climbed Minya Konka (24,900 feet) during one of the most successful high-mountain expeditions of our generation. Other members of the party were William P. House, a brilliant young rock climber, who with Fritz Wiessner had first ascended Mount Waddington in British Columbia in 1936, after sixteen previous parties had been unsuccessful. Next was Paul K. Petzoldt, rancher and guide from Jackson Hole, Wyoming, well known for his climbs in the Tetons and Wind Rivers in Wyoming, and for a double traverse of the Matterhorn made in one day. Capt. N. R. Streatfield, who had been transport officer of the French expedition to Hidden Peak in 1936, directed porter operations; and the writer, who had climbed Mount Lucania (17,150 feet) and other peaks in Alaska and the Yukon, completed the climbing party. Six Sherpa porters were taken.

After being turned back from reaching Savoia Pass by steep ice, the 1938 party, reconnoitering in several teams, was also stopped on two routes leading to the West Ridge of K2, and again on the Northeast Ridge, before making a determined bid on the southeast rib where the Duke of the Abruzzi three decades before had pressed his attack. House and Petzoldt's good reconnaissance work over fretted ribs of rotten rock interspersed with snow gullies brought them eventually to a campsite, later known as Camp II, at 19,300 feet. House and Houston continued the reconnaissance and Camp III was set up at 20,700 feet. This camp proved very dangerous, however, for falling

---

*Burdsall died on Mount Aconcagua in Argentina (22,835 feet) on February 20, 1953, after climbing the mountain and making a futile effort to descend to help rescue two Italians exhausted near the summit.

stones struck two of the three tents there, one of them while all three high-altitude Sherpa porters were in it. Petzoldt and Houston led up over a short but difficult overhang to place Camp IV at 21,500 feet, below a cliff. Here, while I belayed him, House made the most important "lead" of the expedition. He ascended a steep, 100-foot gash that has become known to more recent expeditions as House's Chimney. More camps were pushed higher until the food supply, depleted by the long reconnaissance, was nearly exhausted. House and I, with the famous porter Pasang Kikuli, helped Houston and Petzoldt to establish Camp VII at 24,700 feet. From there they had food enough to push their way to the foot of the summit pyramid, and Petzoldt reached a height of approximately 26,000 feet before starting down. A more extensive food supply might have permitted this expedition to reach the summit, but a large amount would have been needed, for stormy weather was coming in as the party descended the mountain. The 1938 team, however, had found a route up K2 and brought back the strong hope that the world's second highest mountain could be climbed.

The Second American Karakoram Expedition, consisting of six climbers and a transport officer under the leadership of Fritz Wiessner, reached the foot of K2 on May 31, 1939. Wiessner, a brilliant rock climber, was best known for his attempt on Nanga Parbat with the Dyhrenfurth Expedition in 1932. With him were Jack Durrance, who had made daring ascents in Wyoming; the experienced veteran Eaton Cromwell; forty-two-year-old Dudley Wolfe; and two young climbers from Dartmouth College, Chappel Cranmer and George Sheldon. With Lieutenant Trench as transport officer, and nine picked Sherpas under Pasang Kikuli, the party reached Base Camp on schedule, and after a brief look at the Northeast Ridge decided to try the route the 1938 party had named the Abruzzi Ridge. Eventually eleven loads were moved up to Camp VII, and two days later Wiessner and Wolfe pitched Camp VIII five and a half hours higher. On July 17 Wiessner with Pasang Lama pushed forward to set up

Camp IX at 26,050 feet, but deep snow caused Wolfe to return to Camp VIII.

On July 18, in good weather, Wiessner and Pasang Lama made a bid for the summit, but difficult climbing slowed them, and finally at 6:30 P.M., when they were well over 27,000 feet—perhaps to 27,500—Pasang Lama anchored the rope and would not let the indomitable Wiessner continue. Wiessner had been planning an all-night climb! During the dangerous night descent that followed, the Sherpa had lost both men's crampons (climbing irons) from his pack. Back in camp at two-thirty in the morning, the two men were too tired to make another attempt next day. On July 21 they tried a different route, but without crampons 400 to 500 steps must be cut—too many for one day. If Lama had not lost their crampons! It was now too late to try the first route again. The chance was gone.

Next day the two went down to Camp VIII, added Wolfe to the rope, and descended to Camp VII to bring up more supplies, but on the way Wolfe slipped, and though Wiessner stopped the fall, Wolfe lost his sleeping bag. When the group reached Camp VII, they found to their horror that the camp had been largely evacuated during their long absence. The reserve sleeping bags had been taken, with the result that they spent the night with only one small sleeping bag and one air mattress for the three! Luckily the weather was still good, and next day while Wolfe remained at VII, the others went down to VI to bring up additional food and sleeping bags so that the summit attempt could be continued. But Camp VI had also been evacuated, and so were the other camps as their descent continued. To save their lives, Wiessner and Lama continued to go down. After a dreadful night at Camp II, the two climbers next day, completely broken physically, reached Base Camp.

The explanation of the stripped camps was that the Sherpas had thought the climbers long overdue and apparently dead. Trying to salvage something, unfortunately they had packed down the precious sleeping bags so painfully carried up.

This was the tragic story of the nearly successful fourth expedition to K2, but their experiences did not discourage the world's mountaineers. Instead, the challenge that had drawn Dudley Wolfe to the mountain had become even greater, and if World War II had not begun, it is certain that the fifth attempt to climb the Karakoram giant would have come much sooner.

2 *Preparations*

ROBERT H. BATES

Grim, stark, dangerous, each time K2 has defeated a team of climbers, it has strengthened the desire of others to take up its challenge. After the Wiessner expedition to K2 was turned back within 1,000 feet of the summit in 1939, Houston, House, and I of the 1938 party began to plan another assault.

During World War II, of course, our return was impossible, but soon after the war ended, House and I called on the Indian ambassador to discuss applying for permission to go to K2 in 1947. We were dissuaded. Then came partition of the subcontinent into India and Pakistan, followed by a struggle of these countries for Kashmir, until eventually a cease-fire line that absolutely nobody could pass was set up across this divided country. The political division of Kashmir seemed to block completely any hope of expeditions to K2, for the southern half of the route was under India's control and the northern part, known as Baltistan, was held by Pakistan.

But Dr. Houston, who had already done more mountain climbing in Asia than any other American, should not be underestimated, for after House and I had given up hope of returning to K2, he became more determined than ever to go. Realizing that to reach K2 without crossing the cease-fire line might be possible, he wrote to a distinguished diplomat and friend of long standing, the Honorable Avra Warren, who in 1951 was the American ambassador to Pakistan. The right man in the right place can do wonders, and despite earlier indications of failure, in the spring of 1952 permission was granted to Dr. Houston to lead an expedition to K2 in 1953.

From then on, we were caught up in a whirlwind. We were disappointed at first when Bill House of the 1938 party decided that his business would not permit him to make such a lengthy trip, but others were eager to go. That spring we talked to George Bell, who was preparing to go to Salcantay in Peru; wrote to Peter Schoening, leader of the King Peak Expedition; and saw or corresponded with a host of others. Selecting personnel was critical and difficult. Who could tell whether candidate X, who had climbed so well in British Columbia, was potentially a better man for the K2 expedition than candidate Y, famous for his rock acrobatics among the Dolomites and his ice work in Bolivia.

Finally we decided to wait until after the summer climbing season of 1952–1953 to select the party; and we agreed on the characteristics we wanted most in members of the K2 "team," for a mountain expedition above all else is just that: a team. It must act cohesively, and there is no place for the brilliant climber who thinks only in terms of personal success. Anyone selected for such an adventure must be a *good all-around mountaineer,* but even more important, he must have that indefinable quality, *good personality,* and be able to keep his good nature and add to the humor of the party when bad weather, danger, or hardships strain the nerves. (High-altitude dispositions are notoriously bad.) Next in importance we placed *expedition experience,* for no number of daily climbs from a hut give the practice in living and working together under trying conditions that one gets from being on an expedition—especially one where the members carry their own loads. Third in importance we put *technical ability* on rock and snow. Probably no major Himalayan peak yet climbed requires such diversity of mountaineering skills as K2. Therefore we could not take brilliant rock climbers if they were inexperienced on snow or men whose climbing background was in any way one-sided. K2 is no mountain for the specialist. Unlike Everest, which is almost entirely a snow mountain on the side by which it was climbed, K2 on the south side is a rock and snow mountain with a wide range of technical problems.

These were the main criteria for selecting the team. We discovered that many of the candidates were overly modest, and in the end we found ourselves with more suitable men than places. Initially we had thought of a six-man party, which had worked well in 1938, but when we learned that we could not take Sherpas, we increased the number to eight. Sherpas had been a help to us in 1938 and had been employed with great success on Everest, Annapurna, and other great Asiatic mountains. Feeling against India ran so strong in northern Kashmir at that time, however, that it seemed unwise to take with us any of these sturdy little men. In their place we should have Hunzas, bigger men, who come from a small, mountainous border state in northern Pakistan. Hunzas have not had the years of expedition training that many Sherpas have had, and therefore we thought it unlikely that they could climb on the Abruzzi Ridge of K2 above Camp II. To compensate for the fact that we should be doing all our own load carrying on the upper part of the mountain, we decided to enlarge the climbing party to eight, with the idea that the carrying capacity of at least eight men would be needed.

If eight men would be better than six, why wouldn't ten or twelve be better than eight? In some ways they would, but campsites on precipitous K2 are scarce. It would be very dangerous, even if possible, to move a group of seventeen porters up to 26,580 feet on K2 as was done on Mount Everest in 1953. Steepness, lack of campsites, and loose rock limit the size of the party. Houston and I agreed on a party of eight and at once began exhaustive letter writing and interviews to help us to decide who the other six would be.

Selecting the party from the numbers of strong and experienced men who wished to go was especially difficult, but the choice was finally made. Our biggest member physically was

6-foot-5-inch, twenty-seven-year-old George F. Bell, assistant professor of physics at Cornell University. Bell had climbed widely, but was best known in the mountain world for his part in the successful expeditions to Yerupaja and Salcantay in Peru. Also tall and a veteran climber was twenty-eight-year-old Robert Craig of Aspen, Colorado, philosopher and ski instructor, whose first ascents of Kate's Needle and Devil's Thumb in British Columbia brought him national prominence in 1947. The Middle West was represented by Arthur K. Gilkey of Iowa, a geologist who was finishing his work for the Ph.D. at Columbia University. Gilkey in the summer of 1952 had directed with great skill the Juneau Icefield Research Project in Alaska, basic glaciological research by the United States government, and was known for his youthful climb of Devil's Tower in Wyoming, and subsequent brilliant ascents in the Grand Tetons.

A climbing companion of Bob Craig of many years' standing was thirty-four-year-old Dee Molenaar, artist, ski instructor, and geologist, who had been an outstanding member of the Mount St. Elias Expedition to Alaska in 1946. Like Craig and Peter K. Schoening, a chemical engineer, Molenaar came from Seattle, but twenty-six-year-old Schoening is the only one of the three still living there. Schoening's climbs on extremely difficult rock were well known before his leadership of the highly successful King Peak Expedition to the Yukon in the summer of 1952. Our transport officer, Capt. H. R. A. Streather of Warminster, England, and our Pakistani member, Col. M. Ata-Ullah, were to join us later.

While personnel problems were being solved, we worried about finances. At least $25,000 needed to be raised, and only part of that sum could be expected to come from the members of the expedition. To assist in solving this major problem, Richard L. Burdsall of Port Chester, New York, a member of the First American Karakoram Expedition, accepted the arduous job of expedition treasurer; then after Burdsall's tragic death on Mount Aconcagua in Argentina, William P. House, another member of the 1938 party, took on the financial burden with great skill. (Eventually, about one-quarter of the money was put up by members of the expedition, one-quarter came from advances on television rights and articles, one-quarter came from loans, and one-quarter from gifts.) Unlike most European expeditions, we were not subsidized by our government, nor were funds given us by any organization. Although the American Alpine Club sponsored our expedition, we used none of the club's funds. Mountaineers and friends helped us out individually, but we did most of our own deficit financing.

While money was being raised and selection of the expedition team was going on, first steps had already been taken in the selection of food and equipment, and as each member was added, he took over some phase of the work. Through Pete Schoening, some fine down jackets, made to the expedition's specifications, were donated by a Seattle firm. Gilkey worked on stoves and Molenaar on some lightweight nylon parkas. Boxes began to pile up in the garage and front hallway of the Houston residence in Exeter, New Hampshire.

Hundreds of decisions had to be made. What type of mountain boots should we use? Should they have rubber cleated soles, or leather soles with metal boot nails, or rubber cleated soles with metal nails? (Each man finally used the type of sole he thought best.) Some boots were made to our measure free of charge by a French firm; others came from England and from Canada; while still others were the rubber, vapor-barrier boots developed by the United States Army. Similar problems concerned gloves, underwear, and even socks. Pete Schoening for instance had socks and mittens made for the whole party by Indians in the Pacific Northwest, but their ideas of size must have been based on ancient legend, for some of them had heroic proportions.

Each man showed some special preferences in clothing. Schoening kept snow out by tying his outer trousers to a tab sewn around the upper part of his boots, while Art Gilkey used puttees for the same purpose. George Bell sported Peruvian hats, while Bob Craig had several colorful headpieces, one with a long red tassel down the back. But perhaps the most treasured items of clothing were a wool helmet and some lightweight underwear made in the Hebrides and saved by Charlie Houston since his first expedition to K2 in 1938.

Food was one of the most important of all problems. Mrs. Houston became accustomed to experimental dinners of dried vegetables, strange soups, and special compounds, some of which were finished by the dog. We tried Antarctic pemmican and honey biscuits, special chocolate beverages from the Rocky Mountains, dried meat bars from Chicago, and several varieties of baby food. The baby-food cereal seemed a good idea, for we needed food that required little or no cooking to simplify life and save fuel at high altitudes. Baby food had simplicity, all right, as we were later to agree, but the simplicity applied to the taste, too, so that we later unanimously agreed that babies have been cheated for years. Once let them taste something with flavor and they will be through with baby food forever.

Finally, after days of experiment with prepacked, lightweight foods and delicacies that had been favored on former expeditions, we settled on the foods we wanted, added one-quarter extra to most quantities to make sure that Pete Schoening would have enough, and started to order. Almost at once the Houston residence began to look like a grocery store. Cases of meat bars—each bar a pound of steak dehydrated to 4 ounces—began piling up at the foot of the stairs, and dried apricots and dehydrated toasted onion soup blocked the route to the garbage can. Mrs. Houston fortunately is blessed with patience, for the Houston children celebrated each new arrival with delight and curiosity, as if a new Christmas were being arranged especially for them.

Finally, when the Houston home had been turned almost completely into a workhouse and the family were considering a sleeping-bag existence in a tent in the yard, the big "packing week end" came. Senior members of the Exeter Mountaineering Club and the Harvard Mountaineering Club and other friends foregathered with some "heat sealers" and large quantities of plastic tubing, for we planned to eliminate weight of packaging and increase efficiency by packing all the individual items of high-camp food into units for two men for one day. The small packets were placed in larger plastic bags, and these in turn in cloth bags, weighing about 28 pounds each, which would nourish eight men for three days.

The "packing week end" was sensational. Assembly lines were set up in the Houston kitchen and dining room. A visiting scholar from India and a visiting educator from Pakistan worked together vigorously and cooperatively, and as the empty cartons piled high, amazing progress was made. In one corner Mrs. Houston's best bread knife was in service cutting twenty-four wheels of Italian *pan forte* (fruitcake) into eight sections each. The knife has never been the same since. In another area, dehydrated potatoes were measured into plastic bags, the air was squeezed out, and the plastic was sealed together by a heat sealer. It was important that these seals be firm, so an inspection service was set up to test the bags for defective sealing or for too much air, which might cause the bags to explode at high altitude. Sample testing grounds were established in the living room, only to be removed in haste to the kitchen when Mrs. Houston witnessed the damage wrought by a few defective bags of powdered potato and flaky baby-food oatmeal. The linoleum of the kitchen floor also suffered, especially from a gummy combination of excelsior and sticky raisins that clung as if cemented in place.

For two days this group worked at furious speed, making plastic containers, heat-sealing them, and packing them in specially made plywood boxes which were to go all the way to Base Camp unopened. Lids were nailed on the boxes and a Harvard-M.I.T. team strapped them with metal bands; then they were numbered, printed labels were stapled on, and the containers were ready for their voyage halfway around the world. During these vigorous days, vast quantities of excess chocolate and sugar-coated peanuts were consumed, and somehow Mrs. Houston provided meals for the whole hungry crew.

At one sitting, a 24-pound turkey, roasted in front of the living-room fire, completely disappeared.

Along with the boxes of food, we packed climbing equipment: 960 feet of nylon climbing rope, crampons (ice creepers with spikes 2 inches long), snaplinks, rock *pitons,* and ice *pitons.* Pitons are spikes which can be driven into rock or ice. A snaplink or *karabiner* (a large snaffle) can then be snapped into a hole at the end of the spike, and the rope secured to it. Our snaplinks were very light ones, developed by the U.S. Army Quartermaster Corps for the use of mountain troops during the war. The ice pitons, of a new design and very strong, had been carefully made for us under the most modern engineering principles by David Bernays, a student at M.I.T. Perhaps the most unusual piece of climbing equipment was a light aluminum A-frame with pulleys, which was to be used in hauling loads past one of the steepest parts of the route.

We also packed two containers of oxygen, which Dr. Houston had obtained from Dr. Ulrich Luft of the Army Air Force for use in case of emergency or frostbite, or perhaps for a needed boost near the top if the summit party could not acclimatize properly. We did not plan to use artificial oxygen as the Everest parties have recently done, not because we considered its use unsporting, but because it is expensive, cumbersome, and introduces many complex problems. A large number of load carriers are needed if oxygen is to be used regularly, and as already described, K2 is not a peak which can support many men at once. Also, if oxygen fails to work when an unacclimatized climber is high, he may even die on the spot. But we knew that at least half a dozen climbers on Everest had reached over 28,000 feet without oxygen in the past and believed that we could go as high. We would rely on acclimatization to train our bodies to live in thin air.

Exposure to high altitude is often uncomfortable. Anoxia seems to drain the body of energy and will, but severe illness on mountain expeditions is a rare thing. Naturally, however, Houston as expedition doctor selected his medical kit with great care, and it was packed and sent out with the rest of the 4,500 pounds of supplies which were to go by freighter to Karachi, Pakistan.

Finally, after weeks of struggle, some sixty-three packing cases were loaded on a truck which would take them to the New York piers, and the Houston garage was freed for normal use for the first time in months. I saw the whole consignment loaded on the *City of Carlisle* in New York on April 23 and returned to Exeter to get ready to fly to Karachi to meet the freighter when she steamed into that busy roadstead of the Indian Ocean.

3 *To the Mountain*

ROBERT W. CRAIG

On the night of May 23 a magnificent farewell party was given by members of the American Alpine Club in honor of our expedition. Older members of the club, on whose shoulders we had in a sense stood in order to gain our own reputation and ability, gathered about us and imparted a warmth of feeling and a spirit of unity that none of us were to forget throughout our whole adventure. Next day a few last-minute dashes from one end of Manhattan to the other netted the expedition such items as half a dozen extra hand warmers, more photographic film, and a tape recorder. At last we all assembled at Idlewild International Airport on the afternoon of Monday, May 25.

Morning found us in London, wishing we could leave the airport to touch elbows with the Coronation crowds, but our stop was hardly long enough for lunch. In the late afternoon we were trying vainly to buy a quick beer in Frankfurt. We then discovered that we could satisfy our thirst adequately on the plane, and even managed to round up a few bottles of an excellent airline vintage for "cold nights in Base Camp." Some weeks later we were to think enviously of those bottles so easy to buy on the plane.

Through the second night we traversed the eastern Mediterranean, and morning brought us a brief but impressive glimpse of Beirut, Lebanon. During the rest of the morning we flew across the northeastern part of the Arabian peninsula and over much of the area where history was being made two millenniums ago.

In midafternoon of the second day of flight we dropped down onto the sun-baked airport of the young city of Karachi, capital of Pakistan. We stepped from the air-conditioned aircraft into a vise of heat which was to haunt us in varying degrees until we reached the cool, dry land of Baltistan far to the north. High-ranking officials of Pakistan and the press greeted us as we alighted. Bill Crockett, administrative assistant to Ambassador Hildreth, was there to help too, and several of his aides. Most important of all there was Bob Bates, who had flown to Karachi ahead of us to convoy more than 2 tons of food and clothing and equipment through customs. Since his arrival he had arranged to have the supplies shipped by rail to Rawalpindi, where they would be flown the last 190 miles to Skardu, the capital of Baltistan. It was wonderful to be together again, and we felt more and more like a team. We now lacked only Tony Streather and Colonel Ata-Ullah. Thanks to our many friends, we were quickly passed through customs, and were soon en route to the American embassy, where we were to spend the night through the kindness of the American ambassador. The air-conditioned bedrooms were most welcome, but even more so were quick baths, in which we removed the dust of half the world. After this we walked through the sticky, humid evening air along mysterious lanes to Bill Crockett's garden, where a party was given in our honor. We found an amazing amount of interest in our expedition, and much of the conversation in the garden that hot, muggy evening concerned mountains. We talked to many Pakistanis who had traveled there, and saw a superb moving picture of the area.

We slept for a few hours, and were up next morning at four to fly via Orient Airways to Rawalpindi, 900 miles to the north. The flight was hardly a scenic one, for much of it lay across the baking Sind Desert, a wasteland of sand uninhabited for thousands of miles, and visibility was limited by a misty layer of dust which formed in the great heat. We landed at noon in Rawalpindi, a city which saw a lot of action in Kipling's day and which has long been a gateway to the Northwest Frontier Province and the western Himalayas.

We were hardly down the ramp of the aircraft when we became aware of the presence of Colonel Ata-Ullah, the Pakistani who was to be our friend and companion on the expedition. One of Houston's principal hopes for this expedition was that it should encourage friendship between Pakistan and America by showing that young country how similar its people are to our own in ambitions, ideals, and abilities. We wanted Pakistan to share in our attempt to climb its highest mountain, and we had looked for a climber and a companion. Thanks to Sir Zafrullah Khan, foreign minister of Pakistan, who had taken a great interest in the expedition from its beginning, the ideal man was found in the person of Colonel Ata-Ullah. Our first impression of him as we left the plane was that of a dynamic individual with great power, great ability, a sensitive intelligence—one who would become our warm friend.

Beside him, equally impressive though not so formidable, was smiling, alert Capt. Tony Streather. Tony was a twenty-seven-year-old officer in the British First Gloucestershire Regiment, who had reached the summit of Tirich Mir (a 25,260-foot peak several hundred miles west of K2) with a Norwegian expedition in 1951. Houston had corresponded with him, their letters had led to friendship, and he had been accepted sight unseen. Within a few days of our meeting in Pakistan, Streather was one of the most popular members. His disposition never changed, he told fabulous tales of Northwest Frontier country, and he always had a story about that part of the world. Best of all, he was not only an excellent transport officer, which was his primary responsibility, but he soon became one of the party's strongest packers and climbers.

We were quickly taken in hand by these two efficient men, both thoroughly familiar with Pakistan, and we and our baggage were transported to the home of Colonel Ata-Ullah, where we were to stay. There we settled back and began for the first time to see something of Pakistan and its culture.

In Karachi our stay had been so short, and so limited to American surroundings, that we could not even begin to feel the atmosphere of the country. In Rawalpindi all of this changed, for we had as guides Ata-Ullah's two sons, Munir and Shahid, as well as his nephew, Masood Ahmed. With them we made excursions to all parts of the city and were told of the age and importance of the various mosques, bazaars, and the historical sites. We toured the oldest bazaars in a jeep, and visited parts of the city we would never have seen on our own. Meanwhile we settled down in Ata's house, and rapidly piled our equipment all over his lawn.

Many vital things had to be done, and we spent most of our time opening crates shipped across the Atlantic, and repacking food and equipment into 60-pound porter loads. Then, too, there were endless and inevitable check lists to go over, and new lists to be made. Some equipment had been damaged and had to be replaced, and some new purchases had to be made. The temperature was usually between 100° and 120° in the sun, and the work came hard.

While our days were, if anything, too full, there was also a considerable demand for our time in the evenings. Many of Ata's friends were anxious to meet the party, and many had a genuine desire to know more about the mountains which protect the northern frontiers of their country. Thus our evenings were spent in a round of wonderful dinner parties, where we met some of the most brilliant and capable of Pakistan's leaders. We ate enormous amounts of strange and delicious Pakistani dishes, and in the cool evenings on the lawn of the colonel's house we talked about mountains, men, and the world in general. We learned about the birth of Pakistan, formed in forty-six days as the result of the partition of western India (predominantly Moslem) and central India (predominantly Hindu) in 1947.

We talked about the problems faced by this the youngest of the world's great nations, and we came to admire deeply the courage, patience, and the energy with which the people are solving these problems.

Our stay in Rawalpindi was packed with excitement and new and interesting things. Houston visited several hospitals and was deeply impressed with the caliber of medical care given. We visited the Signal Corps training laboratories built up from nothing by Colonel Young, an English officer on duty with the Pakistan army. We made courtesy calls on the ranking officers of the Pakistan army, and were honored and pleased to be invited to return. All of this made our week in Rawalpindi an Arabian Nights adventure. But K2 was ever present in our minds, and we were drawn irresistibly by our future.

June 1 broke hot and clear, and in the earliest light of dawn we could see the blue Himalayan foothills shouldering above the misty plains. Trucks had carried our $2\frac{1}{2}$ tons of equipment and food to the airport the night before, and all that remained was to say good-by to our kind hostess, Begum Ata-Ullah, collect our scattered possessions, and drive to the airport to begin one of the most exciting flights any of us had ever experienced. The flight to Skardu probably exacts more skill from a pilot than any other regular air route in the world. Capt. Henrik Franczak of Orient Airlines, who had been a pilot in the Polish Air Force and later in the British Air Force during World War II, told us about the flight which would take us through the foothills, over several 13,000-foot passes, flanked on either side by great mountains, and alongside such giants as Rakaposhi, Haramosh, and Nanga Parbat, all of them over 25,000 feet high.

We left soon after six o'clock, with the heat of the day already beginning. It was a relief to ride above the baking plains, and fly over first the brown, arid fields which merged into gradually greener hills, steepening slopes, deeper gorges. Then appeared a little snow here and there, larger patches, glaciers, and then the great rock and ice kings themselves. Visibility was not always good, but we saw enough of certain peaks to be convinced that we were among mountains that must be classed apart from all others. Our plane was joined by a second Orient Airlines plane which flew wing to wing with us through the rugged gorges, past mighty Nanga Parbat, which the Germans were so soon to climb.

All the time we flew among these fantastic hulks, the plane had painfully little clearance over ridges, summits, and between narrowing walls of the deep gorges. Abruptly we cleared one final ridge, saw the widening valley floor of the Indus, and in a sickening dive we seemed to plummet toward the ground. At the last moment the plane leveled off, skimmed some deep gullies, and touched down on the hard earth of the Skardu landing strip. We had arrived! In only an hour and a half we had reached Skardu, where the 1938 K2 party had arrived after a 220-mile trek, during which they had marched the equivalent of the distance from Boston to New York in two weeks.

We drove off to the village in jeeps, leaving our equipment to follow under the care of the Northern Scouts, a local levy of smart and capable mountain soldiers. To our astonishment we were met on the way about a mile from town by a huge delegation. Lined up along the sides of the road were all the school children of Skardu, cheering, throwing flowers, and waving banners to welcome us. There were speeches every few hundred yards, garlands of fresh and fragrant roses were placed about our necks, and the crowds cheered, *"Pakistan zindabad! America zindabad!"* (Long live Pakistan! Long live America!) Placards urged us to use our influence with the United Nations to see that a Kashmir plebiscite be held. Other banners thanked America for the gift of wheat. Still others welcomed us to the wonderful country of Pakistan. We felt that our welcome was a sincere demonstration of the hospitality of these people toward strangers, as well as a symbol of the affection felt by these people toward America, half the world away.

Changes had occurred since Houston and Bates had been in Skardu in 1938: then the 2,000 inhabitants had been cut off almost completely by distance from the outside world; now we heard that there were 7,000 people in Skardu, and as many more in the surrounding villages. Much of this increase can be attributed to the influx of refugees from Kashmir, and to the presence of the Pakistan army in Skardu. Also, the city had become more accessible because of the airlift, which supplies it completely with all its needs: jeeps, oil, food, equipment, as well as such luxuries as they have. Perhaps most significant for the future of all the changes in the orchard-fringed capital of Baltistan was the addition of a modern hospital, complete with a small electric-light plant and a movie theater. These developments were owing mainly to the work and patience of the chief surgeon, Major Khan, who had come back to Pakistan after twelve years of medical practice in London. He was to help us immeasurably in the months to come by his presence in Skardu.

In the few days we spent in Skardu, the final packing had to be done, and the porters had to be chosen, arrangements made for forwarding mail, and schedules set for radio messages to us. We greeted our Hunza porters, who had marched fourteen days from the distant and famous valley of that name to serve as mountain porters for us. They had been selected by the Mir of Hunza, and we had no idea how much they were going to mean to us in the days which lay ahead. Between our preparations we were lavishly entertained by all the officials of Skardu, and managed to take in such sights as the ancient Skardu Fort (reputed to be 500 years old) and the lovely lake of Satpura. All of this activity took place in a setting of vast open plains of sand along the speedy, muddy Indus River. In the distance, precipitous, multicolored rock peaks capped with snow looked down on irrigated fields and orchards lined by graceful Lombardy poplars. Here the Baltis grow barley, wheat, millet, apricots, mulberries, apples, and peaches. In the evenings we relaxed on the lawn of the summer house which was formerly used by the Maharajah of Kashmir, a beautiful garden on the edge of a steep cliff which falls sheer for hundreds of feet to the Indus River plain.

At last all of our preparations were completed, and early in the morning of June 5 as light faintly touched the highest peaks above the Indus Valley, our "bandobast" (porter caravan) started down the steep trail to the river. There we were ferried across the mile of muddy, rushing water in an ancient wooden craft not unlike our canal barges. This vessel is attributed to Alexander the Great, and is said to be the very barge in which the great Greek conqueror led his armies across the river. Whether or not this is the very vessel he used, it probably is a similar model, and uses the same means of propulsion. The shallow, rectangular barge is certainly primitive enough, and is moved across the river by water power with a minimum of paddling. Starting far upstream on the Skardu bank, where most of the townspeople had gathered to say good-by, each boatload of thirty or forty men and baggage pushed off into the current and was carried downstream at a terrifying rate. Only disorganized attempts to guide the barge were made by the four boatmen who wielded long oars in a style far removed from our regatta at Poughkeepsie, and yet we finally reached the far shore in safety, a third of a mile below our starting place on the opposite bank. The process of hauling the barge upstream and making the return journey took some time, and we were glad that most of our porters had crossed the night before. About a hundred and twenty-five porters stood back from the river with their loads arranged in a long line. Loads and men were checked, and then at a signal each man slung his 60 pounds on his back and we set off across the hot, dazzling sand of the old river bed. Our march had really begun; we were on our way to K2!

For the next fourteen days we plunged farther and farther into a land of fantasy. Beauty is not a term one generally can apply to Baltistan and the Karakoram, although certainly there are places where intense beauty confronts the traveler. Rather the land is one of harsh yet magnificent contrasts: immense rock spires soar thousands of feet to glistening ice summits, while below the stark brown monotony of parched earth and sand is broken only occasionally by roaring glacial torrents or emerald-green trees and fields of a village. These villages hang onto precipitous slopes and are made fruitful by painstaking irrigation. Wherever a small side stream falls from the mountain, generations of natives have built long ditches to bring the water to the terraced fields. The climate of Baltistan is pleasant: warm in summer, and not severe in winter. The mountain vistas are incomparable. The menaces of "civilization" seem far away. These people appear to have a heaven on earth, and perhaps they do, and yet for all of this they live in hovels of mud and straw like those used by their ancestors for the past 1,500 years. They are dirty, and their sanitation is nonexistent. Illness is common. Houston, as a doctor, could not help thinking aloud what wonderful changes could be made with even the simplest principles of cleanliness and public health.

There is a kind of magic which sometimes kindles when men are joined together in a common effort, and this seems particularly true in mountaineering. In the vast reaches of the Karakoram the experience is not restricted to the climbers but infects the whole expedition. The porters are not there for the money alone—it is hard and dangerous cash to earn—but because they too feel caught up in the spirit of the hills and the hunger for adventure. Particularly this is true of the mountain porters, in our case the Hunzas, who feel themselves set apart and above the baggage porters.

As day after day of hard marching passed, the porters began to form a solid group, and the whole expedition shook down together. Not only did the porters and the climbers come to know each other, but we climbers, most of whom had been strangers at the start, came closer together. Our various temperaments began to show, and we began to learn each other's good points and peculiarities. Only Bates and Houston, and Molenaar and I, had climbed with each other before. The others were comparative strangers. As we approached our mountain, the magic cement that binds men together, the qualities which make unbreakable friendships began to form. Unconsciously, and imperceptibly, we were forming a team. If we had not it is probable that most of us would not have survived the troubles that we were to face. Perhaps it is these bonds, formed of success and failure, that make mountaineering expeditions—like all ventures of man into the heart of nature—such a rich, emotional experience.

A typical day on the march to the mountain began when the Baltis began to murmur as the dawn chill pierced their blankets. Village sounds drifted through our camp (we were usually camped in an orchard near a village), and Vilyati (our cook, sirdar, and mountain porter) began preparing eggs and chicken bought from the villagers, or cereal, tea, and meat from our own stores. Try as we would to withdraw deeper into our down bags, these noises soon woke us and we crawled out of our tents saturated with ten hours of sleep, to breakfast at four-thirty. Blisters and stiff muscles made the start painful, but first we had a long and complex period of load sorting and assigning. The daily consumption of sahib and porter food necessitated each morning a reshuffle of loads, and some crafty porters often tried to carry a bulky pack which looked as if it weighed a hundred pounds, but was in reality only twenty-five.

Unfortunately not all of the Balti porters felt "caught up in the spirit of the hills," and much of our time during the march was spent encouraging the laggards—giving a cigarette here and there, or shouting encouragingly a word which sounded like *"shabash"* (well done), which was usually sufficient to keep things rolling along.

Lunch was eaten along the trail at about eleven, and after this we usually marched until three-thirty or four to our camp-site. From Skardu to the snout of the Baltoro Glacier is about 100 miles, and the days were blisteringly hot, the sun relentless. Soon after the porters straggled into camp our cook would produce what passed by the name of tea—several quarts of strong brew, crackers, jam, cheese, fruit, and a tin of sardines or kippers. We would barely have time to finish this feast before dinner was served, but there never seemed to be any difficulty in finishing this meal too. Dinner consisted of dried vegetables, soup, tinned meat or local chicken, pudding, and a hot drink. We sat around our tent or campfire until seven or eight o'clock, talking easily and happily on topics ranging from home and family to the day's march and the character of our new friends, or world politics and philosophies. In the middle of a learned discussion someone would break in with his thoughts on the subject dominant in all our minds—the mountain: "If we can't find a safe place for Camp III, protected from rockfall, will we be able to manage the long climb from II to IV in one day?"

Some of the days brought more dangerous tasks than plodding over boulder-strewn alluvial fans. There was, for example, the river crossing between Bahar and Niyil, about halfway from Skardu to Askole. The porters claimed that the old route on the right bank of the Braldu River had been destroyed by avalanches, and urged that we cross the turbulent river. At the place selected for crossing, the river is divided into two parts by a sand bar. The first and smaller part was forded through river water which rushed waist-high. It was necessary to fix a handrail to help the lazy porters across, but even so a few preferred to return home. Once on the sand bar all porters and loads were collected in one place, while we watched the crossing of the larger half. This was done on a goatskin raft, a *zahk,* made of some thirty goatskins lashed together by a light flexible framework of split poplar poles. The resilience of these rafts, their seeming weakness, gives them strength, which was important in the turbulent water. Only four passengers and loads could be taken at a time, and all the porters prayed with great emotion before boarding the raft and tossing off into the high waves. Their fears were justified, too, for the icy river churned and boiled down through a narrow race with waves 1 to 2 feet high. The crossing was a tedious process, taking us a day and a half to get all the porters and their loads across.

Two more days' march up the valley we came to another river crossing, even more trying on the nerves. This was one of the infamous "rope" bridges of the Karakoram. These bridges are made by twisting pollarded willow shoots and twigs together into thick strands, two for handrails and one for a footwalk or treadway. The bridges sag deeply from the high banks on either side as they span the river at a narrowing point in its bed. Apparently they are placed in position during the winter when the river is either very narrow or frozen. They are replaced only when broken, and they sometimes turn upside down, pitching the traveler to certain death in the mauling, freezing waters below. One of these bridges actually did turn over with one of our porters on it, but he was so terrified that he did not let go, and the bridge was righted and he was saved. One other unpleasant characteristic of the bridge is for the two handrails to come together and squeeze the traveler like a vise, unless a man remains in the middle of the bridge to hold the cables apart. We had three of these miserable things to traverse, each seeming worse than the last, and many porters parted from us at each one. Fortunately, however, no one was lost, nor did even the most rickety bridge collapse.

Just below Askole, the last village we would pass, we enjoyed the long anticipated pleasure of a bath. Here a series of natural hot springs flowed out of the mountains, at precisely the perfect temperature for bathing. The natural pools have been only slightly improved by the local people, who seem to have no use for them. We enjoyed complete privacy as we soaked, up to our bearded chins, for several hours, with snow-capped mountains hanging almost over our heads.

In Askole we bought more flour, hired more porters, and enjoyed half a day of restful camp life. We were quartered in the village park, a shaded meadow surrounded by poplars and briar hedges. During the afternoon various members of our caravan and villagers broke into a spontaneous song and dance, much to our delight. Many hundreds of spectators watched and applauded as natives from different villages competed for the most impressive dance. The singing of Baltistan has a certain falsetto quality, and is mostly in half notes, but it is most pleasant and fascinating.

In the morning, our departure from Askole was signaled by a tremendous uproar as we collected porters and weighed out flour to feed them on the way into the mountain. Everyone wished to come, and every man wished to furnish his own flour. Much confusion resulted, and it seemed as though we would never get away; yet order was finally restored.

A short distance beyond Askole we left the path, no longer dignified by the name "beaten," and began the last five days of marching to the Baltoro Glacier. Our campsites were primitive, and lacking in firewood, which was a handicap to the porters. One day we were caught in a gigantic dust storm, which nearly blew away our tents; on another a sudden rainstorm overtook us and almost drenched our equipment. It was with mounting excitement that we rounded a great bluff and looked at the Baltoro Glacier, one of the largest in the temperate areas of the world. A great, ugly mass of ice, dirty and gray, covered with millions of tons of rock and gravel, filled the valley floor.

We had some trouble in climbing onto the glacier, and once on it no trail existed, for the rock, sand, and gravel which cover it are constantly shifting as the ice moves down the valley. The lower part of the glacier is occasionally visited by local people who seek wood along the side slope or who bring their goat herds to high pastures. Their visits are so infrequent as to leave few marks, but two recognized campsites have been developed on the shore. Our marches were slow and laborious, covering little more than 6 miles during eight hours of walking and climbing.

On the first day we reached Lilipru, a small, flat area on the shore, surrounded by vertical cliffs, where an ancient glacier had carved a channel. On the next day we walked an even longer march up the gully between the mountain and the glacier to Urdukas. This would be the last grass we would see for two months. It is a beautiful campsite, a series of grass-covered ledges, great boulders, and deep caves. It served as the Base Camp for the Duke of the Abruzzi, and also for the Duke of Spoleto, who camped here in 1929. Many mountain sheep and goats, snow leopards, bears, and wolves live here, the last game in the valley. We spent a happy afternoon in the grass and among the beautiful Alpine flowers, surrounded by incredible peaks above and about us. I wrote in my diary one day: "Scenery grows more fantastic as we progress—these are hardly mountains: they are fantasies of the imagination." At regular intervals along both sides of the valley blocks of rock, often capped with ice, rose vertically for 8,000 feet, for all the world like mammoth skyscrapers. Houston, who has been in three different areas of the Himalayas, stated that nowhere else had he seen peaks like this, and certainly none of us had seen their equal.

We then crossed the glacier, making two cold and uncomfortable camps on the ice before we reached the great open place called Concordia, where many glaciers flow together to form the Baltoro. Finally, about ten o'clock on the morning of June 19, we rounded the corner where the Godwin-Austen Glacier, flowing from the north, enters "Concordia." Here we expected to have our first glimpse of K2. Instead a great bank of clouds separated the high—the impossibly high—summit from its base, and gave us a tantalizingly brief view of the summit pyramid, high above the clouds. New snow covered most of the mountains above us, and a formidable wind spewed a long snow plume from all the summits. We could imagine the force of the wind that was lashing the upper slopes of K2, and we knew that before long we would be testing its might. Little was said at the moment, but we all realized that we were joining battle with a tremendous foe.

After this brief, imperfect, yet striking, view, clouds again covered the mountain as we marched up the last miles to Base Camp. Snow began to fall as the tired porters straggled into camp late that afternoon. Our long approach was at an end. The monarch of the Karakoram rose high above us, and the real work of the expedition was about to begin.

4 *To the Foot of Abruzzi Ridge*

CHARLES S. HOUSTON

Only a few inches of snow had fallen during the night, and we awoke on June 20, in Base Camp at last, to a perfect day. About us rose magnificent peaks sparkling in the clear, frosty air. Bride Peak was particularly lovely at the foot of the valley, her pure snow peak dyed by the sun with many colors. Directly above our heads, pile upon pile, towered the southern wall of K2, a series of precipices of rock and ice reaching to a white snow cone 12,000 feet above. Our porters, so miserable during the snowfall the night before, were all smiles and laughter as they woke, and buzzed around camp in their ragged brown cloaks, which resembled nothing so much as burlap Mother Hubbards. Two of the most exhausted and weak had been allowed to sleep in one of our mountain tents, and now to our surprise at least six men came out of that same tent. The independent Satpuras, who had built neat platforms of flat stones with a low surrounding wall to keep off wind, had fared well, and even had a surplus of wood to use for cooking breakfast.

Camp was soon humming with activity. Streather was anxious to pay off the porters as soon as possible, not only to start them early on their long march home, but also to clear camp of the confusion of the curious, itchy-fingered natives, so he and George Bell settled down at one end of camp to count out the amounts due the men. Each porter was called forward and asked for the metal tag given him upon "enlistment." His name was checked against our list, and our calculated amount was given him. Many of the porters had never before seen money, and their bewilderment was comical. They were obviously determined not to be cheated, but they had no conception of the value of the bank notes. An apparently fundamental rule of human conduct was not violated: however much you are given, ask for more. To pay off all 180 men, who came from a dozen different villages, each with a different amount due, took all morning, and then there were arguments and discussions about underpayments. Once paid they were reluctant to leave; they had been so long with the circus that they hated to miss any tricks.

In the meantime the rest of the team was not idle. Our small, two-man mountain tents were pitched in a neat military row along a flat stretch of glacier covered thinly with small stones. Behind and below the tents, a small brook flooded a gully during the day, but was reduced to a trickle during the cold of the night. Our tents faced the towering rock cliffs of Broad Peak across a waste of ice and rock, while down the valley we looked upon Bride Peak, grim Mitre Peak, and a score of lesser, unnamed summits. The kitchen tent was pitched on a platform in the gully near the brook. The Hunzas enthusiastically hacked out of the ice a neat footpath, complete with giant slabs of rock to bridge the stream. Our supplies, covered with tarpaulins, were stacked here and there about camp, while the Hunzas had their own tent off to one side. It was a wild and barren spot, with no blade of grass or even a patch of earth, only ice and rock about us. It would be our home for nearly seventy days.

Bates and Craig and Gilkey had set out in the early morning to reconnoiter the icefall between Base Camp and Camp I, while Schoening, Ata, and I unpacked supplies and organized camp. We had some shocks. Many of our 5-pound Cheddar cheeses were broken or crushed. Some of the chocolate had melted and mingled with other food. Tins of sardines had been punctured. Several tents were badly chafed, and the holes had to be patched. Two porter ice axes were "missing," and nowhere did we find the boots belonging to Tony and the porters, which had disappeared during the river crossing.

Soon after noon the reconnaissance party returned, freshly burned a brilliant scarlet by the reflected white heat of the sun against the ice, and reported having reached Camp I without difficulty. A good route had been found through the icefall, several routes in fact, and the passage, although tedious and hot, was not difficult. We celebrated their accomplishment with a special brew of ice-cold Jell-O, which revived Molenaar, who had been confined to bed with fever and weakness.

During the afternoon each man was given the special high-altitude clothing he would need, and each sorted and re-sorted such personal items as books, mittens, "snorkels" (a type of breathing tube made from the upper 6 inches of a woolen stocking and worn over nose and mouth), and bright and fanciful caps. From here on we would be limited to 40 pounds of clothing and gear per man, and cutting down came hard to some. George Bell, our ace photographer, objected, "How about this three-foot telephoto lens for my Leica? Does it have to be included in my weight allowance with my other cameras and their film?" Schoening and I, with movie cameras and tripods, were sympathetic, and finally cameras were allowed in excess, as was film.

Over tea, which dragged on into dinner, we discussed plans. We had reached Base Camp despite frustrations, worries, and delays, within a day of schedule, losing only a small amount of food and equipment. The theft of Streather's brand-new boots was a serious problem, and we would also have trouble in finding mountain footwear for the Hunzas to replace those boots which had been stolen. Apart from these minor worries we were in good shape, well and strong and ready to go.

Tony's report on the treasury was not exactly reassuring. After paying off the porters he was able to muster four annas, approximately eight cents, and this only after each individual had given up all his own funds to the expedition treasury. This sorry financial position seemed unimportant among the splendid peaks which surrounded us, and with our own mountain squarely above us. I knew we would have mail runners to pay, however, to say nothing of the wages for the forty-five men who would return from Skardu on August 10 to carry home our equipment. I put the worry away until tomorrow, and we talked over plans.

There are three main ridges on K2 reached via the Baltoro Glacier approach: the Northwest Ridge, a steep, long rock ridge which plunges directly from the summit to 21,870-foot Savoia Pass; the 5-mile-long Northeast Ridge, a fearsome knife-edge of ice with fantastic towers and cornices, which runs from the summit pyramid down to Skyang Kangri; and the Southern Ridge—Abruzzi Ridge, which is a cluster of rock ribs in the steep southern face rather than a discrete and separate ridge. Bates and I saw no good reason to doubt that the Southern Ridge was our best choice. Our inspection of the Northeast and Northwest Ridges in 1938 had convinced us that they were not practical routes to the summit, nor did we fancy the avalanche-swept precipices between these tremendous ridges. Wiessner's party in 1939 had also chosen the Southern Ridge after inspecting the others.

Nor was it difficult to decide upon campsites, for there is not much choice on K2. Camp I would be near the foot of Abruzzi Ridge, far enough out on the glacier to be safe from avalanches. This would be reached by a tedious march through the crevasses of the upper Godwin-Austen Glacier. From Camp I to Camp II we would follow the route found in 1938, for Camp II was too good a site to bypass. Camp III presented a serious problem. In 1938 we had narrowly escaped injury on several occasions when rocks dislodged by climbers above had fallen through our tents, once even knocking a cup from the hand of an astonished porter in the old Camp III. This had been a poor site, cramped, exposed to wind and stonefall. This camp we must either bypass or place differently. But could another location be found on that ever-dropping slope? If not, the section from II to IV would be a long and difficult climb, perhaps too long to be done in one day. Camps IV, V, and VI could be located in their old sites. Camp VII we felt might be placed somewhat higher, though this was uncertain. Camp VIII would obviously be placed near the foot of the summit pyramid, while somewhere in the rocks less than a thousand feet from the summit we hoped to pitch Camp IX, a small bivouac tent with food for two men for three days.

Our task was to build a pyramid of food and supplies up the mountain, with its apex resting at Camp IX. In order to accomplish this, between 1,200 and 2,000 pounds of food and equipment would have to be carried to Camp I, with smaller amounts to each of the higher camps. It was imperative to leave food and fuel and some equipment at every camp to provide a reserve at each in case we should be forced to retreat during storm.

For this task we did not have much carrying power. Thanks to the help of the Mir of Hunza, we had brought with us from Skardu ten excellent Hunza porters. We intended to keep six or eight of these with us on the mountain, feeling confident that some would choose to return home with the other porters, which proved to be the case. The six strongest remained with us to serve as mountain porters. To be sure, the word "mountain" applied to these tough, cheerful fellows was a misnomer, since only one of them had ever been on a glaciated mountain before. They were strong, however, courageous, energetic, and willing. With the training we had given them on the march in we hoped that they would develop into capable climbers. These men would help us to carry loads at least as high as Camp II, and possibly to Camp III. Above this the terrain would be too difficult, the campsites too cramped, and supplies too limited to take them higher.

Base Camp was a busy place. Upon our arrival it seemed the wildest, most desolate, most remote spot in the world. Within a few hours it became home, and when we came down to it from weeks above, it seemed a luxurious resort. Our tents were pitched on a thin moraine, only a few inches of small rocks covering the snow, with tall, white ice cliffs on either side. The heat of the sun, when the sun did shine, beating upon the glacier, melted the ice beneath its stony cover very rapidly, whereas the tents protected the ice beneath them. As a result we found our tents "rising" above the glacier at the rate of some 6 inches per day. Each week they had to be removed to another site, or else a ladder would have been necessary to reach them.

Reorganization of our supplies was not complicated. All of the "soft" rations, such as cereal, sugar, rice, and fruits, had been carefully packaged in Exeter, and one day's supply for two men packed in plastic bags. To these bags there now remained to be added only tinned goods, and the other "hard" articles. This packing required time and some ingenuity, and even so we were later to find some bags that had an excess of one item or lacked another. Our work was cheered by the discovery of photographs, notes, clippings from magazines, pin-up girls, and other items from home, inserted by our packing assistants and our families. Our afternoon was not untouched by nostalgia.

The following days were filled with activity. Large amounts of food and supplies were gradually carried up to Camp I, sometimes in the burning heat of the sun, which turned the glacier into a white-hot furnace, but often in a cold blowing mist of snow and wind which chilled us to the bone. On the hot days we found ourselves plowing through slushy snow, falling into hidden lakes and rivers. On cold days we walked firmly on the crust and often wore crampons.

After returning from the daily pack trip, there were many chores about camp to be done. Molenaar professed to have had experience as a barber, which his sample demonstration did nothing to confirm. There was little choice, however, and most of us preferred to have our hair cut by a "hack" than not to be clipped at all. Bathing was a slipshod affair because we did not think we could spare fuel to heat water, and the only other available water was that which flowed in the glacial stream at a temperature a tenth of a degree above freezing. We went off on several short exploring trips across the glacier or around the corner toward Savoia Pass, but we did not climb any of the lesser peaks around Base Camp because we felt that acclimatization would proceed satisfactorily during the packing period without other climbs. In retrospect I think that this was something of a mistake, and I now believe that on a subsequent trip a period of a week or ten days might be allotted to climb smaller summits from Base Camp, thereby increasing the thoroughness of acclimatization.

Our evenings "at home" were spent in writing letters, making tape recordings, and sorting food and supplies for Base Camp. Ata was now determined that he would remain at Base Camp while we were on the mountain. Since we had become more and more fond of him, we were loath to send him packing homeward. As he pointed out, it was obvious that he could be of considerable help to us in Base Camp, and his cheerful support and energy would be invaluable. There was the complication of finding supplies for him, however, since we had brought no great surplus for ourselves. Bates, in charge of the commissary, was somewhat dubious, but finally conceded that there would be plenty for Ata if we were all careful. The die was almost cast; it appeared that he would remain.

Wild life at Base Camp was scarce, but curiously enough a half-drowned squirrel, or at least a member of the squirrel family, came floating down the brook one afternoon. He was rescued by the Hunzas, restored to life with a little food, and after playing around camp for several days set off jauntily down the glacier. What this poor animal was doing at 16,500 feet where no natural food could possibly be expected is still a mystery. There were many birds about camp, mostly of the chough family.

Here and there among the rocks on the mountain itself, and less frequently in a tiny patch of sandy soil on the glacier, we saw small primula of the most gorgeous colors. A few spiders and flies were apparent on the hottest days, but in general there was very little animal or plant life in this remote and barren land. We saw no trace of the "Abominable Snowman," that half-mythical ape or man alleged to live only above the snowline in the Himalayas. Tracks were not seen, nor did we hear any noises, smell any odors, or see any shapes which might have contributed to the notoriety of our expedition.

So the days passed. The initial lassitude, shortness of breath, and slight headaches which most of us had experienced upon arrival at Base Camp disappeared within a few days and we felt stronger and more eager every day. The Hunzas, too, were gaining more confidence in glacier travel as well as in the curious white-skinned sahibs whom they followed. The weather seemed to smile upon us; the mountain appeared to welcome us. How little we knew of what lay ahead!

5 *The Attack Is Launched*

CHARLES S. HOUSTON

All the peaks about us were glittering in the cold, clear dawn on June 26 as I broke the skim of ice on the little brook before the cook tent and started breakfast. This was to be the great day when our attack would begin.

Bates and I were to move up to Camp I, from there to examine the route to Camp II, while the others carried supplies to I. Once we had found the route to II, another pair would move to that camp while the rest packed up supplies. And so we would creep up the steep slopes: reconnoitering, establishing camps, packing supplies, and reconnoitering still higher. In about five weeks we hoped to have ten or twelve days of food at a camp around 26,000 feet, from which to push a party of two within striking distance of the summit. All lay ahead of us on this shining day: all the work, the excitement, the joy—and the heartbreak.

There were many last-minute details to attend to, and not until after ten did we set out, Bates and I carrying extra-heavy packs. Tony and Bob Craig and all the Hunzas were to have a rest day in camp.

The first part of our march lay along the edge of an enormous fan of avalanche debris deposited by the spring snowfalls. This was slushy by the time we crossed, so that we sank to our knees or blundered into lakes and rivers hidden beneath the snow. The upper icefall was hard work in the hot sun and Bob and I, tailed out behind the others, regretted the added books, the extra socks, the little specialties we had tucked into our packs. We reached Camp I—still only a cache—by midafternoon and sent the others back to Base while we pitched the tents and settled down.

With sunset the cold fell upon us like a blanket, and a bitter wind blew up the valley. At six I put on my warmest clothing and set out a few hundred yards to the lip of the icefall, where I could have direct line of sight with Base Camp to try out the radio. Tony Streather's cheerful voice came in on the stroke of six-thirty, and I was much relieved to have such excellent contact. I rejoined Bates, walking gingerly across the crevassed glacier, and we settled down in our tents.

The next morning was beautifully clear. We hurried through breakfast, examined our prospective route through field glasses, and fumbled through the maze of cracks and séracs (ice towers or pinnacles) to the "shore." Then we started up Abruzzi Ridge. For the first two hours we climbed steep scree (loose stone) and snow slopes, crossing a few little ribs, exclaiming "I remember this chimney" or "Do you see that cairn? I'm sure we must be on the old route." We could see the snow slope below Camp II tantalizingly above us, but we could not seem to find the route to it. Over and over again we hopefully worked up a ridge or gully, only to come to an impassable section and retreat.

By noon we had to confess that we were lost. Climbing over increasingly loose and exposed rock, we simply could not find the old route. Far below we could see the rest of the party crawling up to Camp I under huge packs, and we returned desperately to our search. Another few hours found us hopelessly entangled with a precipitous gendarme (a rock pinnacle) and, at last, rather than retrace our steps, we admitted defeat and started directly down a gully to the glacier below, a route that had nothing save directness to commend it. About five we straggled into camp, freshly burned by the hot sun beating on the rocks, footsore, weary, and most embarrassed.

"How did you experts make out?" greeted us as we arrived.

Bob and I exchanged glances, each waiting for the other.

"Well, we couldn't seem to hit on the 1938 route. We worked across a couple of gullies and over two main ridges, but then we couldn't find a way over or up the big ridge that you can see leading up to Camp II," I said. "On this side the slabs are pretty easy, but the whole damn thing overhangs on the other side. I don't know how we got over it before."

"I think we were too high," said Bates. "I think we ought to cross that gully low down and go up the scree slope all the way. Remember that long, miserable slope?"

"No," I argued, "the big gendarme on that overhanging ridge must be crossed high. The lower part is worse than the upper. We have to get onto the Camp II ridge higher up. We were much too low." The others laughed at us, and we retired in some confusion.

Next morning George Bell, Bob Craig, and I set out to tackle the upper route, while Schoening, Gilkey, and Bob Bates took the lower; Streather and Molenaar went down to Base Camp to bring up a last relay of loads. About eleven someone called, "Look, isn't that a rope?"

"Yes, and here's an old piton and another cairn. This must be the old route for sure."

We crossed a gully, puzzled over some intricate towers, toiled up a loose, steep slope to a chimney, which I certainly recognized, and finally there was Camp II before us. Our shouts reached the second rope far below and they started back to Camp, Bates first doing a spectacular lead through a keyhole in a ridge which was little thicker than his body.

We found lots of surprises here: several dozen tins of jam and pemmican scarcely rusted in the thin air, some gas containers, stoves, and best of all, a Logan tent carefully wrapped and sheltered beneath a tarpaulin. We couldn't resist pitching the tent, which to our surprise was in good condition despite its fourteen years of exposure, and we turned back to Camp I happy in the realization that Camp II could thus be said to be "established." We joined the others on the descent and spent some time in fixing ropes over some of the more airy passages, especially across the smooth, worn slabs in the gullies, and reached camp after four, tired and more than ready for the thick brew of Jell-O which had become our standard "afternoon tea."

The early evening was broken by the shouts of the Hunzas, who had been sleeping massed together like sheep in one of the large tents, and suddenly rushed out into the darkness calling, "Sahib, come quickly; you must get up. The glacier is cracking. Camp will fall into a crevasse." The groans and creaks of the ever moving ice had scared them badly and it took some persuasion to get them back to bed.

The wind howled in a crescendo toward morning and snow beat upon us; yet we managed to pack loads and start out, hoping at least to get more supplies part way. Though the visibility was poor, we worked our way up to the tent platform built in 1909 by the Duke of Abruzzi, where the 1939 party had established their Camp I. Huddled in the lee of those rocks, we decided to leave our loads there. Returned to camp, we passed a happy afternoon in bed, reading and writing letters, while the wind—there was little snow in the scudding mist—played about us.

June 30 found all of us, Hunzas and sahibs together, packing 40-pound loads to Camp II, a round trip which took us nearly eight hours. Ata made the trip for the first time and was tremendously enthusiastic. "Charlie," he said as we reached the snow hollow, "Charlie—I'm going to spend the night here."

"No," I said, for, having an inkling of his plan, I had purposely not brought any sleeping bags on this trip. "What would you sleep in?"

"In the Logan tent with a stove and my down jacket I'll be fine," was his reply. But I would have none of this, and the others equally disliked the thought of leaving him there alone, so down we all went.

We were a bit strained that night, probably having forced the altitude too fast. Only two weeks previously we had left Urdukas, now 6,000 feet below. I was distressed by the length of the pack to II, and felt that we could not manage so long a day regularly. We discussed moving Camp I up to the old Abruzzi site, using that as our jumping-off place, but decided instead to try a few more days on our present plan. From the Hunza tent came groans and pleas for medicine. Headaches, backaches, nausea, and generally low spirits indicated that they, too, were feeling despondent. A joint council of war and generous doses of aspirin for all hands put us all in a better humor for early bed.

Now Bob Craig and Art Gilkey would take over the lead, and we all packed up to Camp II, leaving them to enjoy the luxury of the large Logan tent the next night. July 2 was especially clear and hot, and the packers from I continued to build up supplies at Camp II. That evening the radio brought gleeful word from Craig: "We found Camp III all right, and it's not too far. We plan to make two trips tomorrow."

"Did you get fixed rope placed?" I asked.

"Well, you don't need too much," replied Craig. "We put in some, and we'll do the rest tomorrow. Most of the climbing is pretty easy, and you can get away without fixing many rope handrails. Art and I were thinking just now that we might even *move* up to III tomorrow." We all thought nothing of this idea, and Bates and I wondered aloud if they really had found Camp III, a doubt which was strengthened the next day when they reported having made the round trip, with loads, in three hours, and in the afternoon having gone back to lay out and attach the rope handrail on the lower part.

We were now enjoying a real stretch of good weather, similar to the corresponding period in 1938 during which we had first reconnoitered the Abruzzi Ridge. Rest days must wait upon the storms which we were sure would come. On the third of July Bell and I left soon after sunup for the glacier below Sella Pass for a detailed telescopic examination of the summit cone. George had brought along the enormous telephoto lens for his Leica, at least five times as large and five times as heavy as the camera itself. Laden with this monstrosity, movie cameras, and

Abruzzi Ridge profile

film, we wound our way through snow-choked crevasses to the foot of Sella Pass, staying well away from Broad Peak's ice cliffs, which avalanched regularly. The chill wind hurried us along to a point about a thousand feet above and 2 miles beyond Camp I, where we sat down to inspect the mountain.

K2 is an incredibly striking sight from this point. The Abruzzi Ridge seems vertical, a tangle of small ridgelets, black gendarmes, and glistening ice slopes. Fresh avalanche tracks could be seen high up, but we were glad to see that few of these reached the base of the steep ice slopes. Through the glasses we could see House's Chimney and could trace our route to Camps V and VI, only to lose it in the forbidding cliffs which form a roughly triangular rock face at the top of the climbing ridge. This grim section, its apex reaching above 25,000 feet, is called the Black Pyramid and contains some 2,000 feet of the steepest and most tricky climbing on the mountain. We filmed for half an hour, and then saw the tiny dots of the packing party working up the slopes toward Camp II. For another hour we lingered, bitterly cold, hoping to photograph a good fall of ice and snow from Broad Peak. But nothing fell, and we finally hurried down to camp to prepare vast amounts of milkshake for the hot and thirsty packers.

Craig and Gilkey were somewhat chastened that evening. They had discovered what we had expected all along: that their previous "Camp III" was in reality only halfway to the real site, and that distant camp had taken a great deal more hard work to reach. However, they had taken two loads all the way, and one pair of loads was halfway; fixed ropes had been placed over the most trying sections below, and the climbers were sure the route would go. We decided to move two more men up to Camp II, and on July 4, which was still bright and sunny, Bell and Molenaar were established there while the rest of us carried up loads and returned to I. Our celebration of the Fourth was mild: a nip from our precious Scotch in which we graciously allowed the Britisher, Streather, to participate. But the day was really made noteworthy by Ata's announcement from Base Camp that mail had arrived, our second in two weeks. Two Hunzas went down to get this next day, and brought Ata back with them.

Now came our first supply problems. In planning an expedition such as this where weight is all-important, where ounces as well as pennies have to be counted carefully, quantities are measured closely. Only a moderate surplus is allowed. In all our supplies we had a reserve of perhaps 25 per cent for unexpected bad luck, a slender margin. During the next two weeks, gas became our main worry. With Ata and the Hunzas steadily cooking at Base Camp (which we had not anticipated in our plans) while the rest of us worked slowly up the route, would our 40 gallons of gasoline be sufficient? Like the Sherpas, the Hunzas are a prodigal lot. Their happy philosophy is: "If there is food, eat it all; tomorrow something will turn up." In their estimation gas was intended to be burned, and for hour after hour their stoves roared. It was time, past time, to stop this. We set up strict gas rationing, but continued to worry.

Camps I through V

Meanwhile the packing was going splendidly. All of us felt stronger each day, and the nasty scree slopes between I and II seemed easier every day. We made better time, halted less often, felt better when we returned to I. Still the splendid weather held; not even a cloud lay over the summit. The sunsets, though lacking the flaming reds and luminous greens so often seen in Alaska, were superb. We felt the great freedom of expedition life. The party was working together smoothly and well.

On the sixth we all assembled at Camp II—four of the six Hunzas in the 1939 Logan tent, the others paired off in mountain tents. Khareel, who was too old, and Ghulam, who had passed a large intestinal worm, had been sent to Base Camp, where Ata looked after them and chafed with impatience to join us. We were still teasing Craig and Gilkey about their "Camp III," but in the meantime loads were accumulating at the real Camp III, the route was safe and well established, and excitement was mounting.

All of us carried packs to Camp III the next day, encountering one of the serious problems of K2—rockfall. So steep is the route, and so directly upward does it lie, that rocks accidentally knocked off by the first climbers fall upon those below. Since

Camps II to III

many thousand feet of climbing lie over loose and rotten rock, it is almost impossible to avoid this hazard. We had faced it in 1938 unhappily, and had realized the danger. Now we planned to move closely together, never allowing a second party to straggle more than a short space below the first, taking advantage of all the natural shelter afforded by cliffs and buttresses.

About noon we reached a large outcrop of rock below and to the right of the old Camp III.

"Charlie," said Bob, "this may be the answer to our problem. Couldn't we somehow dig in our tents beneath this overhang, and avoid the exposed campsite we used in 1938?" This was a good suggestion, because the old Camp III had been placed on the open slope, directly in the line of rockfall from above. Several times in 1938 stones knocked off by climbers had whizzed through camp, tearing tents. We had finally taken down the tents each day and covered them with stones for protection, and I had expected that we might have to skip Camp III entirely, moving from II to IV in one long day. But Bob's site looked pretty small.

"Maybe," I agreed, "but we have a lot of construction to do to put two tents here." The eye of faith prevailed. Hidayat led the others in a furious burst of construction. From all over the slope big slabs and small were tossed to the masons in the gully. The job seemed hopeless for several hours, but we all worked with vigor, and by late afternoon a solid revetment nearly 10 feet high had been built up the gully to end in a platform about 5 feet wide and possibly 8 feet long. Above this rose a slight overhang, which would keep off rocks falling from above; below the long steep slope dropped clear to the glacier below.

Meanwhile a second crew was hacking away at ice and imbedded rock on a little outcrop, and bursts of profanity were punctuated by cheers as stubborn stones were broken away. A good platform was finally built there, more exposed, for on each side the rocks fell away steeply, but at least both tents were safe from stonefall from above.

This tiny camp was spectacular. We looked directly across at Broad Peak—still well above us—and down 5,000 feet and perhaps 5 miles away to the gracefully curving moraine where Base Camp lay hidden. Masherbrum dominated the eastern view, just as Skyang Kangri filled the western side. Hundreds of lesser peaks, unnamed, unmapped, unknown, lay before us. I have always been fascinated by the wasteland that lies to the southwest. There the peaks bear very little snow and few glaciers, but stand in stark black and red and yellow aridity, 5,000 square miles of unknown country where little rain or snow falls, vegetation is almost unknown, and no people live. At dawn tiny wisps of cloud floated over these dry valleys, and their deep, shadowed scars accentuated the peaks above. Always my favorite was Masherbrum, its distinctive triangle usually wearing a snow plume.

The shadows were longer and the cold more bitter as we hurried down to Camp II, well pleased with our day's work. After supper, which each tent pair cooked themselves, we drew lots and thus selected Bell, Bates, Molenaar, and me to move up to III the next day. Over the radio Ata asked if he might come up with another load of mail to Camp I, and Gilkey and Craig planned to go down from II to meet him. All went smoothly. As usual, those to be residents at the higher camp found their packs much heavier and larger than expected (the sleeping bags were very hard to compress!), and it was a relief to settle down that night in the two tents pitched on the cramped platform at III. The day was cold with a very high overcast, and gray clouds were thickening in the east. Masherbrum was covered. The radio warned "storm." But July 9 was still good, though cloudy again. Bates was feeling poorly because of an abscessed tooth which had bothered him increasingly for ten days. We forced him to stay in camp, full of codeine, while Bell, Molenaar, and I eagerly started for Camp IV. Schoening and Streather were to make a late start from Camp II, reaching the foot of the open slope not earlier than noon, by which time we hoped to be out of the zone where we would kick stones down upon them. From twelve to two the slope would be theirs, and only after that would we start down. In this way we hoped to reduce rockfall danger to a minimum.

Above Camp III there are two short, steep snow slopes, up which we slowly kicked a staircase, fixing rope handrails freely. We found two caches of pitons and lots of old and rotten fixed rope left by the 1939 party. We moved slowly, feeling the altitude. Soon we were among the steep, broken rock which Bates and I recalled so bitterly from 1938. Molenaar, feeling strong and eager, led off to the left and soon had us spread-eagled over a most disagreeable rock face, clutching small holds and cursing "Molenaar's Madness," as the pitch was obviously christened. Once back on the ridge we worked on up to the front of a big gendarme, a rock tower known to the 1938 party as "Petzoldt's Overhang." Having spent many hours chilled to the bone on a narrow ledge while belaying others up this pitch, I remembered it well from 1938. I pointed out the flake, the ledge, and the overhang up which the route lay—a bit of gamesmanship made unnecessary by the obvious old fixed ropes. George Bell led up this section neatly, but it took time and hard work, and we were glad to rest above it before climbing some disagreeable down-sloping slabs to Camp IV.

There another surprise awaited us. The wreckage of the 1939 camp was all about us—tents reduced to shreds, several large Thermos flasks, fifteen or twenty tins of jam, pemmican, powdered eggs, and a large tin of Ovaltine half used but still in perfect condition after fourteen years. Two stoves, several cooking pots, some gasoline, and three good sleeping bags were also there. Though the sleeping bags were frozen and filled with ice, we were able to dry them out and would bless them several weeks later.

Camp IV lies directly beneath a great vertical cliff of ferruginous limestone from 150 to 400 feet high. This seems to be a great dike or intrusion, standing sheer and steep across the climbing ridge like an enormous wall without a gate. In 1938 we considered it the key to the whole climb, and spent some time in trying to pass around the lower end—an impossibility. Bill House, supported by Bob Bates, finally worked out a spectacular route up a narrow vertical crack, doing about 150 feet of very difficult climbing. House's Chimney was made practicable by many pitons driven into the rock crack, and by hundreds of feet of fixed rope. Once above this obstacle we had felt in 1938 that the hardest single stretch of climbing was done, but while above it we had always worried about getting down safely. To descend that chimney in a storm might well be impossible.

I remembered this chimney with awe, and had wondered about it for many months. During the past ten days I had been mulling over different schemes which would put me in position to try this lead myself without being too obviously unfair to my companions. Now the time had come and I hesitatingly turned to George and Dee, both more competent climbers than I. "Would you fellows mind too much if I tried to lead this?" I tried to make it sound offhand, but they must have sensed the eagerness behind the words, for they both agreed readily.

With considerable misgiving I led off, first up the steep snow to a little rock island, and then across an icy traverse to the base of the chimney. For the first 30 feet I worked on the face, clutching at tiny holds, and trying not to appear too clumsy to the experts below. More by luck and will power than by good technique, I reached the deep cleft, where I huffed and puffed, all the while pretending to get out pitons, adjust the rope, or blow my nose. The upper section was strenuous, though not too difficult. With considerable exhilaration I reached the top finally, and shouted to the others, "Come on up; I've got you belayed like a house." Remnants of the 1938 and 1939 ropes were here in the chimney, both too rotten to use, but both frozen too tightly in the ice to be removed.

This accomplishment meant a great deal to me, for I had secretly feared that House's Chimney would be beyond my ability. I felt that somehow I had crossed the line, that having done this I could do anything above. It was one of the great days for me.

From the top of the chimney one has about 300 feet of disagreeable snow and rock slope to Camp V, disagreeable because it is steep, exposed, and very slippery. At Camp V we found nothing but trash and platforms for three tents. By now the ominous clouds were dark gray and we hurried down to Camp III, delaying only to fix ropes in the chimney and on Petzoldt's gendarme. At III I found Streather established in my tent, for Craig, having brought up more loads with all the Hunzas, had then escorted Bates down to II, leaving Tony in his place.

Bob's tooth was bothering him enough so that he was ready for its extraction, but the dental forceps were in the medical stores at Base Camp, and I was at Camp III. After some conversation on the radio, it was arranged that Craig would go down to I, taking with him Hidayat, who was having trouble with bladder stones, a common ailment in this country, there to meet Ata coming up with the forceps, novocain, and a few odds and ends from Base. With another Hunza, Craig would then come back to II while I came down from III to perform the operation. The day had been a full one for all of us, and after making these plans we crawled into our warm sleeping bags with great satisfaction.

A sense of urgency began to penetrate our thoughts. Up to this point the climbing had been relatively easy, the weather mostly fair, and the altitude barely noticeable. The next few weeks would bring success or failure to our efforts, and each day would become important. We must waste no time. Our supplies, painfully carried up so high, must be used to the greatest advantage. Plans for each day were carefully weighed. We were entering our crucial period—those few weeks toward which a year of hope and work had been aimed. How long would the fair weather last? Would our good health and our acclimatization continue? Our talks, our thoughts, our diaries, and our letters home became more serious.

The weather was still fairly good on July 10. Bell, Molenaar, and Streather started early to carry supplies to IV, while I waited in camp for the packing group from II, who could reach me only after the upper party had left the slope of loose rocks above. It was a pleasant, slack morning. I fussed about camp, drying all the sleepers as best I could, counting our food bags, figuring plans, and often just sitting, wrapped in the immensity of my surroundings.

My reveries were interrupted by the arrival of the party from II, who urged me to hurry down before the truce was over and stones began again to be knocked down from above. Leaving Tony Streather in my tent, Gilkey and I climbed down, reaching Camp II just as Bob Craig came up from I with dental forceps and mail. After a leisurely tea, I assembled my equipment for the first dental extraction of my career, somewhat embarrassed by Mohammed Ali, who, despite his lack of any training, was reputed to be a very proficient tooth puller in his village. He was said to be so good that natives came from long distances to consult him. As I boiled up the forceps and prepared my syringe of novocain, his attitude all too plainly was, "What's all this fuss

Camp IV,
below House's Chimney
(view steeply up)

about? Why not let me take care of this simple business while you get on with the main job?" Clearly my prestige was at stake. With Bates seated on a comfortable rock, his head pillowed in Craig's lap, I injected novocain, carefully seized the offending tooth, and to my intense relief and surprise, with one great pull obtained the tooth intact. The Hunzas were astounded, and from that time on I had considerable stature with all. Bates felt immediately better, and after a few days of Aureomycin was quite restored to his usual happy and energetic self.

In the meantime, Bell, Schoening, and Molenaar were carrying loads to Camp IV, now almost completely stocked. Ata had returned to Base with the unhappy Hidayat. The six o'clock "news" from Ata brought the report of Beria's arrest by Malenkov, but it also brought warnings of storm, which meant much more to us in our present situation. The clouds really burst upon us that evening, and heavy snow fell all through the night. Bates and I, enjoying the unaccustomed luxury of individual tents, found the snow piling in about our heads through our tent door openings, and breakfast next morning was disorganized and unpleasant. The storm, though not severe, continued all day. We lay contentedly in our tents, reading, writing letters and diaries, and enjoying the first rest in over two weeks. The Hunzas, too, seemed quite happy, piled on top of each other in the crowded Logan. Radio contact that evening reported that all was well at Camp III, although the wind was more disagreeable in that exposed site.

This was our first real storm. The Karakoram Range lies beyond reach of the monsoon, which so limits the climbing season on Everest. But as on all mountains, occasional storms occur here all through the summer, and the higher we climbed, the worse these storms would be. A week of storm above Camp VI or VII might put us in real danger. Trapped in our small tents by fierce winds, or unable to move up or down because of the danger of avalanches of fresh snow, we would consume our precious supplies, exhaust our strength. Herein lies the real difference between climbing in the Himalayas and climbing in the Alps. "Rush tactics" are too risky to use on great mountains. One must painfully build up supplies, stocking each camp, ready to live through days of immobilization during these great storms. To climb in storm above 23,000 feet is to court disaster. Frostbite is swift and insidious in the thin air at great altitude. Cold and exhaustion bring accidents. Judgment fails and disaster follows. The mild storms of late July made each of us more acutely aware of weather and its influence on our destiny.

Although nearly a foot of snow had fallen and the weather was still cold and windy, we set off on July 12 to make a final pack to Camp III, waiting until Bell and Molenaar, who were moving up to IV, should have climbed above the danger zone of rockfall. It was a nasty trip. The new snow made each foothold and handhold a problem and cut our speed in half. We floundered in some places, and felt precarious in others. The rock ridges and towers on this part of the climb protected us from avalanche danger, but small waterfalls of powdery snow fell over us, filling our footsteps, hiding the rock handholds. Gilkey and I were glad to settle down at III while the others hurried back to II before the cannonade, signaling the descent of Schoening and Streather from IV, should begin.

We parted from the Hunzas with honest regret. They had long since become a real part of the team, and their climbing had improved each day, until they now seemed thoroughly reliable. Their early cockiness, bred of ignorance, had been succeeded by overcautiousness, which in turn was being replaced by the confidence which comes of knowing the problems and your own ability to solve them. After their initial demoralization at Camp I (and what mountain porters have not gone through this?), they had performed splendidly. We discussed the possibility of taking them higher, but discarded the idea for several reasons. First was the character of the Abruzzi Ridge. Such campsites as had been found in 1938 and 1939 were cramped and scarcely gave room for even three or four tents. We saw little prospect of lodging more than six or eight men in any camp, nor was there much chance of finding better sites. Secondly, so continuously steep was the route that stones knocked out by climbers above raked the entire route below. Parties had to climb very close together, or take shelter while the higher party was working. To have more than six or eight men on the mountain at one time, we believed, would expose the whole party to considerable risk. Nor had we equipped our porters with food or clothing for the higher altitudes, and we did not have sufficient gas, stoves, tents, or food to give to them and still maintain the reserve necessary for a safe retreat for the larger party. Most important of all, we knew that they had much to learn, and might well become liabilities on the harder rock work above when altitude had dulled their reactions. Considering all things, we thought it wiser to send them down to Base Camp with Ata and to carry the packs ourselves. We parted sadly, after exchanging many embraces and prayers. Before they disappeared below the large buttress at Camp III, we heard a last cheer: *"America zindabad; Pakistan zindabad!"*

The next day, another gray, cold one, found us all moving loads up to IV, while Bates and Craig escorted the Hunzas down from II to I, where Ata met them and returned to Base. George Bell and Dee Molenaar carried loads up House's Chimney, and worked on the platforms at V. It was a depressing day despite our accomplishments. The weather had not cleared completely after the storm as we had expected, and more storm was obviously coming. We were close to our planned timetable, but the continued wind and cold was wearing on us all. The sense of urgency quickened.

About midnight great gusts of wind awakened us. Snow hissed upon the tents and sifted in the ventilators. Tony Streather and I discussed the storm sleepily and then dozed off; nothing could be done. Sometime later I dreamed vividly that I was being frozen between two blocks of ice, compressed harder and harder as the blocks froze together. I awoke in a panic, tried to sit up, felt a firm cold wall against my nose. It took a few seconds to collect my senses, to realize that snow had drifted in between the tent roof and the mountain wall, pressing down and out, flattening the roof over our heads. With great effort I wriggled toward the center of the tent (I was on the inner or mountain side), arousing Tony. The wind beat great blows against the fabric; the tent ridge sagged dangerously.

"The poles will break if much more snow piles on the roof," said Tony in a matter-of-fact voice. I disagreed. "The cloth will tear first, or else we'll be crowded off the outer edge. We've got to shovel."

"In this wind? There isn't room to stand outside, and besides, it's pitch-dark. Let's wait until morning," said Tony. But in another half hour we had to decide: shovel or be buried. We drew straws; I lost, and wriggled out of my warm sleeping bag, feeling very sorry for myself as I tugged on stiff, cold boots, parka, and mittens. We slept now in most of our clothes. Muttering and complaining, I opened the tent zipper and faced a wall of snow which I finally cleared away. This gave me a few square inches to stand on while I shoveled and pushed and cursed. Fumbling my way in the howling blackness, I took half an hour of the hardest work to shovel off the accumulated snow, tighten guy ropes, and clear the tent. By then I was wet with sweat and melted snow, thoroughly out of sorts, and glad to crawl into the tent. I did not lose the opportunity of brushing a little fresh snow in Tony's face to emphasize what a hard time I had had. (Once before I had been caught in a half-buried tent, in the high camp on Nanda Devi in 1936. But there the shoveling was easy, for there was space to walk around outside the tent.) Bed was most welcome as I crawled in, and I enjoyed it the more when Tony took his turn at shoveling around dawn. The second tent, exposed on the ridge, had no such trouble, for the wind, although worse there, kept the snow blown clear. Over the radio Camp II reported heavy snow, and Ata chimed in with news of at least 6 inches of snow clear down at Base Camp. Bell and Molenaar had no radio at Camp IV, but I was confident that their location would be safe.

All through the day and night of July 14 the snow blew about us, and Tony and I took turns shoveling out our narrow tent every three or four hours. We read, we slept. Dinners had become real occasions, because our appetites were still good (they were to fail higher up) and considerable ingenuity was usually exercised by the cook. Sometimes he added Triscuits to the boiled meat bars, or fried raisins to the chicken. Sometimes we had oyster stew (minus oysters) by mixing Klim, butter, salt, and tuna fish—a delicious concoction adapted from the "Klim Skardu" of 1938. Bates and I had noticed recently that our companions, heartily sick of our everlasting reminiscences, were now again showing interest in these memories, particularly when they involved some of the epicurean dishes then conceived.

The second night of storm was less severe, but July 15 was clearly another rest day. More than 20 inches of snow was measured at Camp II. Once again we dozed and read, talked lazily, nibbled on hoarded raisins, nuts, or chocolate, and shoveled every four hours. Our schedule was further delayed, and we worried again about our prospects for the summit. That night saw an end to our troubles, for the wind dropped and the stars appeared. We all slept well, hoping that finally the scudding clouds of the last ten days would be gone. But no hot sun greeted us in the morning; instead we found more overcast and a chilling wind. We were determined to waste no more time if possible, and so we made up heavy loads and began the laborious struggle through deep snow to Camp IV. Tony and I felt the chill immediately, and did not move as rapidly as those ahead. By the time we reached Petzoldt's Overhang, we were thoroughly chilled. There we decided to leave our packs, and hurried down to Camp III. Schoening and Gilkey, made of sterner stuff, pushed through to Camp IV, where they joined Bell and Molenaar, whom they found snugly established and none the worse for the storm. No snow had accumulated on that exposed slope across which the wind swept furiously.

Below us Bates and Craig were trying to pack loads from II to III. All morning they struggled through waist-deep snow in the gully above Camp II. By noon both were thoroughly chilled and wet, and wisely they returned to camp. The six o'clock radio contact brought us the startling report of a real "air raid" at Camp II. Craig had left his air mattress on the rocks to dry, while he packed up to Camp III. When he and Bates returned, they found the mattress deflated—with seven jagged puncture wounds. At a loss to explain the damage, they finally realized that the angry chough which was screeching around the rocks had dive-bombed the mattress, thinking it a tasty morsel. These birds are quite large, with a wingspread of 3 to 4 feet, look something like ravens, and often fly as high as 25,000 feet. They have voracious appetites and are incorrigible scavengers about camp, but this was the first time we had heard of them eating rubber. Craig, with a few choice words, hoped that the bird had the bellyache; the mattress, though repeatedly patched, was never again the same.

On the seventeenth our long awaited good weather seemed to have arrived, and we all worked furiously in the bright, calm daylight. Those at Camp IV moved loads up House's Chimney, using an ingenious device made in Seattle by Schoening. An A-frame of tubular aluminum, about 6 feet high, was firmly anchored atop the buttress. Through a pulley at its apex a long doubled rope was led to a second pulley anchored on the small rock island in the snow slope below the foot of the chimney. Loads were tied to one of the ropes and hoisted to the top. This was hard work, and time-consuming. But it was nowhere near so hard as carrying loads up the narrow chimney. This work continued next day while loads were relayed up from III by the rest of the party. On the nineteenth, the gray, cold weather returned. Our spirits sank. We managed to establish the whole party at Camp IV, with most of the supplies for the higher camps already up at V. Tony Streather, George Bell, and Bob Bates and Pete Schoening climbed House's Chimney once again and moved up to V late that afternoon in the hope that all of us working together could finish lifting the six or seven hundred pounds up the chimney the next day. This we did despite intermittent snow, cold, and wind.

Ata reported that night that mail runners had arrived two days late, having been unable to find Base Camp in the storm, and asked if we wanted to send out letters. Each of us wrote a brief note which I read over the radio to Ata, who copied it down, adding an explanatory paragraph of his own. What a sense of isolation this little episode gave us all! It would be two weeks or longer before these messages reached a post office, and another week before our friends received them. By then our destiny would have been resolved, our success or failure would be history. For one of us this would be the last message home. "Camp V, by radio to Base Camp, July 19." The letters comforted us and warmed us, but we felt the more removed from civilization.

We were a week behind schedule by now, but the supply train was well enough laid and we had enough food with us and in the camps below to be reasonably safe—unless the storm should continue several weeks more. However, the constancy of bad weather, the continual wind and cold and blowing clouds had a depressing effect upon us. Gone were most of the jokes; the banter had become more serious. We were more determined now than ever, but the picnic was over; the true struggle had

V
"Claustrophobia perch"

begun. Gas rationing had been profitable and gas was now in long supply, but a new shortage had developed: matches. As the altitude had increased, we had had more and more trouble lighting our excellent little Army stoves, sometimes using ten or twenty matches for one lighting. From home we had brought what seemed to be an enormous supply, recalling the shortage of 1938. Having a surplus, however, during the march in, we had generously given many away here and there to the natives, for whom matches are a great luxury in place of their customary flint and steel. No one had paid much attention as the match supplies dwindled, but now a hasty count showed only four or five hundred left to last us for at least two more weeks on the mountain. For many nights I dreamed of matches and we used many tricks to save them—like lighting a candle in a tin can from which to relight the stoves when they sputtered and blew out—as they often did. But matches were to remain a worry for the next ten days.

7

Steep Rock and Steep Ice

CHARLES S. HOUSTON

High cirrus clouds again hid the sun on July 21, but we all packed loads to Camp VI, the route having been scouted the day before by Bates and Schoening. Above Camp V lie first several hundred feet of steep, loose rock, then an upward traverse across a gully choked with loose snow. Here several ropes of two elected different routes, some high, some low, and soon each pair was vainly extolling the merits of his choice above that of the others. Each party, though, had trouble getting onto looser and looser rock plastered with new snow, and steeper and more difficult pitches. It was a great relief to get onto the ridge itself and to see Camp VI above. Here, at about 23,500 feet, we noticed the altitude more. Only a few hundred feet of loose scree lay below Camp VI, but this steep slope seemed endless as we puffed up to the old platforms first built in 1938, and used again in 1939.

Bates and Schoening had prepared us for the moving sight that confronted us there. On two small platforms nestled under a big overhang lay the wreckage of the last camp which the heroic Sherpas had used when they tried vainly to rescue Dudley Wolfe, sick and alone at Camp VII. Two tents had been torn to shreds. A stove, gasoline, and sleeping bags, rolled and ready to be strapped to the carrying frames, lay nearby. A small bundle of tea wrapped in a handkerchief lay inside an empty stove box beneath the snow. As we dug through the wreckage, we tried to imagine that day, July 28, 1939, when Pasang Kikuli and Tsering had climbed from Base Camp to Camp VI, an incredible climb of 6,800 feet in one day, to join Phinsoo and Kitar, who had come up from Camp IV in the attempt to rescue Wolfe. On the thirty-first, Kikuli, Kitar, and Phinsoo went up to Wolfe again, leaving Tsering at VI. There he had waited for them alone for two days before returning to Base Camp. The others were never seen again. Whether they fell trying to bring Wolfe down or whether they were lost while going to him nobody knows. Whatever their fate, the history of climbing has no braver story, no more generous chapter than theirs. Their sleeping bags, and the pathetic bundle of tea, were sad reminders of their courage.

But we had our own work to do. After rummaging through the wreckage, we left our loads and returned to Camp V early in the afternoon. Then Streather and Gilkey started down to Camp II, where they planned to meet Ata coming from Camp I with Korean boots for all of us, mail, and more fixed ropes. I went down with them as far as Camp IV, where I was to spend the night alone before helping to hoist a few more loads up the chimney in the morning. It had been a long, hard day and I slept well despite the rising wind. After the loads had been hoisted up Schoening's aerial tramway next morning, I joined the others at V, belayed up the chimney by Bell, but the wind was too high to work more that day. Down below, Gilkey and Streather were climbing up from II, having exchanged news with Ata. We worried about them as the storm grew worse, hoping that they would spend the night at Camp III. Bell and I went down to the top of House's Chimney to look for them during the afternoon, and again about sunset, when we saw them through the driving snow. Obviously they were far too cold and tired to join us in the storm, but they managed to collect enough energy to climb to the bottom of the tramway and tie on a small packet which we hoisted. It was precious mail, which brightened the evening for us.

All through the next two days and nights the storm howled. Tony and Art had a radio at Camp IV, and we were able to keep

good contact with them and with Ata, who had by now returned to Base. But there was nothing else to do save lie in bed,
reading, dozing, and talking lazily. I couldn't help recalling Tilman's wry remark on Everest: "The chief danger faced by the
mountaineer at great altitudes is bedsores." As the hours passed,
we thought of the future. We had no worries about getting
down, even if it were necessary to climb through the storm. But
the weather was steadily deteriorating. Each week seemed worse
than that before. We could have no hope for the summit if this
should continue. Yet we were determined to press on. Bates and
I recalled this same week in 1938, when the party was making
its highest climb in hot, fair weather.

Dawn on July 25 was unforgettably beautiful. Tags and tat-
ters of clouds shredded by the high wind lay scattered in the
valleys below. Infinite myriads of tiny ice crystals sparkled in
the air about us. The sky was deepest blue. Across the valley
below us range after range of unknown peaks faded to the
horizon. The rising sun colored all. But it was cold, terribly cold.
Slowly we dug out our supplies, made up our packs, and set out
for Camp VI. The wind numbed toes and noses, and within an

hour we had all had enough, dumped our loads, and hurried back to camp, where we found Gilkey and Streather, who had moved up from IV. Next day it was still cold, but the wind had fallen, and the others moved Bell, Craig, and me to Camp VI to examine briefly the route ahead.

Directly above us was a steep tower, which we climbed on the right, the hard way, for we later found an easier route to the left. Above this, we followed a narrow, upward sloping shelf, and by some gymnastics gained the ridge again. For a while we could work a way up this tiny ridge, forced sometimes off to one side and sometimes off to another. Once we came to a short, slightly overhanging buttress, which was climbed by a spectacular wriggle up and over a granite needle some 10 feet high. Gradually the ridge emerged into the relentless steepness of the Black Pyramid. The rock was solid, steep, polished by icefalls through ages past. The holds were small for hands and feet, and often choked with ice. Bell, who was leading here, was in his element. He spoke very little, moved with deceptive slowness, but never seemed at a loss for the way. Sometimes Craig or I took over the lead to relieve George of the labor of kicking steps in some short, snow-choked gully. Despite the threatening sky, the ceaseless wind, the cold, it was climbing at its best. Seldom easy, seldom obvious, the way required skill and care and engrossed all our attention. The day wore on. It was too cold to stop to eat. Indeed for hours on end there was no place to stop save on narrow footholds where handholds were uncertain. We found no ledge on which to sit for nearly a thousand feet.

Finally, tired, cold, but excited, we reached the upper end of the Black Pyramid, where the slope eases a bit. Snow piles in here and some ice freezes on the slabs, making treacherous footing. Up a narrow gully below a huge boulder we crept, one at a time, carefully belaying each other. This took more time, and by then I was almost too cold to move. Urging the others to climb on only far enough to find a possible site for Camp VII (we had seen nothing even remotely possible so far), I unroped and tried vainly to warm my frozen body on a cramped ledge beside the boulder. For what seemed an eternity Bell and Craig climbed on, clear to the beginning of the green ice slope which we had crossed in 1938. I shivered, not too hard, for my ledge was narrow. Only a few feet beyond, a great precipice fell away to the ice slopes which slid 7,000 feet to the glacier below. Suddenly I heard through the wind roar a warning shout, then another. Small rocks whizzed past, then a huge one. I could see nothing as I clung to my shelter. The cannonade stopped but I dared not stick my head out. When Bell and Craig finally returned, both looked shaken. "I had a little spill," was George's laconic answer to my anxious question. "Little spill my eye," said Craig. "George stepped on a big rock the size of a barrel; it turned under his foot. That's when I shouted to warn you. Then down he went, sliding on his face. I saw him claw at the ice slope with his ax and finally he stopped—a beautiful self-arrest. And a good thing too, for I was in no place to stop a fall."

"Pretty slippery spot," was George's only comment as I roped in and we started down.

The return to camp seemed endless to me, and I was happy to collapse in my sleeping bag under the tender nursing care of the others, who had moved up from V. Bates took charge of my hands and feet and I was filled with hot drinks, but it was more than an hour before I became warm.

The wind made climbing next to impossible on the twenty-eighth, and again we idled in our tents. The afternoon was made memorable by a great conference in Craig's tent, where six of us piled in together until the walls bulged like an overstuffed pillow. Discussion of the next move led to reminiscence of things past, and soon Tony got off on tales of the frontier. For several hours he regaled us with accounts of intrigue and adventure, with near escapes and capture during the war years, and the hectic summer and fall of 1947 when India and Pakistan were divided. It was an exciting afternoon, for Streather has seen much and is a born raconteur. At supper time we regretfully crawled back, each to his own tent, in a real gale. The radio message from Ata that night brought word of the signing of the Korean armistice, but also warnings of more storm to come. Fortunately the warnings did not completely materialize, but high cirrus clouds next morning showed that the storm was still not spent, although the wind had dropped, and we carried 35-pound loads up to the cache near the tentative site for Camp VII in dubious weather. The added new snow made climbing difficulties even worse, and we all felt the cold bitterly.

At last on the thirtieth of July the sun shone hot and warm, and the sky was cloudless. The long awaited spell of good weather had arrived. With high hopes we made up heavy loads. Art Gilkey and Pete Schoening were to move up to VII, and we carried enough food and supplies to insure their safety there. With the large party and heavier packs, we made slow progress, each rope delayed by the belaying of the party above. As the hours passed, the sunlight grew fainter, high clouds came in again to hide the sun, and the wind rose. In the middle of the afternoon, cold and tired, we reached the ice slope where Camp VII should be placed. Vainly we searched for some spot where the "eye of faith" might see a tent platform. In this sloping waste of rock and ice we found nothing. A few small stones were there, but not enough to build up a wall, and nowhere could we find snow deep enough to carve out a ledge. It was far too late in the day to try to cross the ice slope to find shelter in the broken séracs on the far side, where we had camped in 1938. All were tired and cold. We were reluctant to retreat with Schoening and Gilkey to Camp VI. As we sat dejectedly on the rocks, Craig chopped idly at the slope. His ice ax broke through; he had hit upon a shallow cave roofed with ice. In a few moments all of us had hacked into the slope and soon a sort of platform was built. It was not the most inviting spot, measuring at most 6 by 4 feet, and floored unevenly with chips of ice. Worst of all, it lay at the foot of a steepening ice slope, which disappeared in the clouds above. New snow on that slope might mean avalanches unless the wind blew it clear. But, considering everything, it seemed reasonably safe to leave Pete and Art here for

Camps V through VII

that night; indeed we had no other choice if we were to proceed higher with the climb. Unhappily, we left them to pitch their tent, and hurried down to Camp VI, where we were much relieved to hear over the evening radio that they were settled in reasonably comfortable style.

By now we had all become reconciled to wind and cloud, although we hoped against hope for the few clear days we needed. I think that by now we had all decided that we must climb in doubtful weather if we were to have any chance of getting higher. To remain in camp, waiting for the long anticipated spell of clear weather which we had every reason to expect at this season of the year, would exhaust our supplies and spell defeat. The seventeen days of food and fuel which we had carried up to Camp VI would, I felt, be sufficient to allow us to push ahead, trying to get in position for our final climb when—and if—the weather cleared.

The thirty-first was definitely not a climbing day, at least not a day on which to tackle the Black Pyramid. Schoening and Gilkey, facing the dangers of a second day at Camp VII, rightly chose to search for a better site. As we lay snugly in our tent, they reported over the radio every two hours. First they managed to cut steps across the ice traverse to the séracs among which the 1938 and 1939 parties had camped. They found the whole area greatly changed and after an hour of search found no adequate campsite. Returning to the tiny tent which we called Camp VII, they next carved steps directly upward until they reached the snow where they could kick a stairway. Up this slope they labored for several hours through the clouds, emerging at last on a flat area on the very edge of the great precipice which falls toward the east and Base Camp. From this campsite they radioed the cheerful news: Camp VIII was found. It would be a long and difficult climb from VI, almost 2,000 feet, but there was no choice. Back to their narrow ledge they went, stopping only to fix ropes over the steepest ice. Theirs was a magnificent accomplishment, carried out under hard conditions, and it made possible all the events, both good and bad, which followed.

August 1—Swiss day. We saw the sun again, through racing clouds which said, "Go on, the storm is over. The sky will soon be blue, the sun warm." Leaving Bates and Streather to follow next day, the rest of us broke camp, taking all save two tents and a little food and fuel with us. We started up the long, hard climb to Camp VIII. Schoening and Gilkey were busily packing food from VII to VIII as we struggled up the last stretch of the Black Pyramid, moving very slowly with our packs, for even 35 pounds weighs heavily at that altitude. Five hours later we reached Camp VII. As we passed the now empty ice ledge, we met Schoening and Gilkey returning through the clouds at VIII to guide us up. We strapped crampons on our clumsy Korean boots, added more supplies to our packs, and climbed on up the huge steps carved in the ice by our pioneers. It was a nasty stretch, pure green ice as smooth as a skating rink, with only scattered stones here and there. We were all frankly relieved to reach the snow, where our footing was secure although more difficult.

I thought that day would never end. I was counting steps, my hope being to climb ten steps before stopping, but I found that I had to stop more and more often. Finally, in the deep snow, I unroped and set my own pace, for the men above seemed tireless. Often the clouds hid them from me, but I had their tracks, knee or thigh deep, to follow. About six o'clock, close to exhaustion, I reached Camp VIII, where a tiny tent in this white wilderness would be our home. The rest were equally tired, but we all managed to pitch two more tents, blow up our air mattresses, cook supper, and crawl into bed. It is surprising even now to recall how quickly we recovered. Morale was magnificent. We were within striking distance of the goal. The summit might still be ours.

We spent a sleepless night with the wind beating about us, but next morning the sun shone hot and full and we dragged out our snow-caked sleeping bags and our wet clothes to dry. Gilkey and Schoening felt miserable. They had shared one of the "impermeable" nylon tents, a fabric which does not "breathe." Both men blamed this semi-suffocation for their illness. Both had severe headaches and felt nauseated. Schoening saw double. Neither was able to do much for an hour or two.

Over the radio I made plans with Bates and Streather at Camp VI to meet them at Camp VII around noon. After enjoying the unaccustomed sunlight for an hour or two, we hurried down to the empty ledge at VII to bring back what few loads of food remained there. The wind and clouds were so bad again that we felt certain that our friends would have turned back. We packed up loads and started upward. Through the storm Craig heard a shout. We listened. Sure enough, a hail from far down the pyramid. They were still coming, but far, far below. We held a hurried conference. Without tents it was too cold for us to await them there. Late as they were, it seemed almost impossible that they could reach Camp VIII that day, and neither they nor we had a tent in which to sleep at VII. They must be sent back to Camp VI. Altogether we shouted again and again, "Go back, go back." The wind mocked us. Finally we started to climb again to VIII, certain that our message must have been received.

But some little voice within reminded me of the strong determination of these two men. From the Camp at VII I gathered up the pile of willow wands, 3-foot wooden dowels painted black at one end. Passing these out to the others in the party, we planted one dowel every 50 feet up the slope as we climbed. This would guide the others if they should come through the snow which had already completely buried our morning track, and would soon hide the tracks we were then making. We arrived at Camp VIII late in the afternoon, thoroughly cold and exhausted. It was growing dark. "They will never come now," said Pete. As he spoke there came a weary shout. It was our friends, exhausted, triumphant, cold, and hungry.

"Yes, we heard your shouts," said Streather. "But we thought you meant *we* are going back." "So we kept on," added Bob. "Thank God for your willow wands. We had no idea where your camp was and couldn't see a thing. Your tracks were completely gone above the ice steps."

While Pete and Art pitched a tent for them, George and I hastily boiled up a pot of tea, only to spill the whole pot as we poured. Our tent floor was flooded, our sleeping bags soaked, but who cared? The party was all together, all well. We had the men, we had the food, we had the will, but would we get the weather? It was a happy evening with high excitement which kept us talking until late.

The night was long and our sleep broken. Battering gusts of wind flapped the fabric of the tent against our heads with malicious force. Snow sifted through tiny holes in the tent and through the ventilators, covering us with powder. Crowded as we were with boots and clothing, food bags, stoves, and pots, there was little room to turn or stretch. Sleep was fitful and broken. The wind screamed about us; snow hissed on the tent walls.

Day broke a sickly gray. No sun penetrated the dense white mist of cloud and tortured snow. Only our watches advanced the hours. Snow piled in drifts about the tents until a sudden change in the wind swept them clear and piled new drifts elsewhere. We were disinherited from the earth, our only horizon the tents. Once or twice during the day a man would move from one tent to another, chat for a while, and then stumble off. But no one could live long in that white hell of wind and

driven snow; fine sharp ice crystals penetrated our lungs, smoth-
ered and choked us. Only by cupping heavy gloves about his
mouth could a man draw a breath. Though it was not terribly
cold, perhaps 0°F., the chill of the tearing wind was bitter and
we were cold even in all our clothing. There was nothing to do
save lie in our sleeping bags, where fortunately we were warm,
and wait—and hope—and wait.

Our one contact with the world, the world of people and
things (not the world of tents and snow and wind), was the
radio. Every morning at seven and every evening at six I took
the wonderful little Raytheon walkie-talkie out of my sleeping
bag, where I usually kept it to warm the batteries. Anxiously I
would wait for the stroke of six.

"Hello, Base Camp. Hello, Base Camp. This is Camp VIII.
Can you hear me? Over." And a cheerful voice would answer,
"Hello, Charlie, I hear you very well. Give me your news, please.
Over."

"Well, Ata, the storm keeps on up here. There is nothing to
see, and we can't get out. But we are fighting-fit and ready to
go. What is your news? Over."

"Here too we have storm, Charlie. Even at Base a foot of
snow fell today. None of the peaks can be seen. The wind is
terrific. Over."

"Ata, tell me the weather forecast." And Ata would answer
sadly, "Charlie, tonight Radio Pakistan said, 'At 24,000 feet the
weather will be cloudy with heavy snowfall. Winds will be west-
erly, blowing 40 to 45 knots, occasionally gusting to hurricane
velocity.' I'm sorry, Charlie, but if the forecast is right, you will
have more storm tomorrow." I could feel the sorrow and the
anxiety in his voice. I knew how he longed to help us, how
powerless this energetic and determined man must feel. But his
presence at Base Camp, his voice on the radio, gave us new
strength.

As we lay in our tents, or visited each other through these
stormy days, our thoughts were always on the summit. Endlessly
we discussed plans. Over and over again we made out careful

lists of the supplies we would carry to Camp IX, supplies for two men for three days. Three days that might give us victory. But three *good* days they must be! Three clear, calm days. On the first day the whole party would move two men to a camp as high as possible on the summit cone, somewhere in the black towers to the east of the ice, perhaps above 27,000 feet. On the second day these two would make their bid for the summit, returning that night to Camp VIII. On that same day a second team would move up to Camp IX to help the first party down if successful, to replace them and make a second try on the third day if they had failed.

"Three days—just three clear days," we said.

August third and fourth were like the first and second. Wind and driven snow. Mist and cloud. Tents flapping against our heads and shoulders. For an hour once or twice in those days we saw a sickly sun, were able to crawl out and stretch our legs in the deep drifts.

Despite the continuing storm, our spirits were so high, our confidence so strong, that we selected the summit teams on August 3. I had anticipated that various factors would eliminate three or four men from a possible summit try, but here were eight climbers, all apparently fit and eager to go higher. The philosophy of our expedition had avoided one-man decisions, and I was reluctant to choose by myself the men who might have the great chance for the crowning effort. We took a secret ballot, therefore, selecting our two best men by vote of all. Each of us thought carefully and long, and when I crawled back from the other tents through the blizzard, I was prouder than ever before of my party. When the ballots were counted, Bell and Craig were to be the first team, Gilkey and Schoening the second. But I asked Ata not to tell their names to the porters when I radioed him that night, for one of our cherished hopes was to preserve the anonymity of the summit pair—if they succeeded. We hoped to report, "Two men reached the top"— no more, no less. We felt that this would doubly underline the team nature of our enterprise. It would emphasize as strongly as we could the interdependence of the climbing party. But this was not to be.

The lulls were rare and brief. During the fourth night the wind gained new force. George Bell and I watched the nylon walls of our tent stretch and pull. Runs appeared in the fabric. We knew that the cloth could not last long.

I wondered aloud, "George, shall we get out of our tents now and make a dash for another?"

"I think we'll last till daylight," was his calm answer. "It will be tough to get into boots and move our gear in the dark."

"Even if we could survive the wind," was my mental note.

So we slept fitfully, and every time I looked up the runs were wider and longer. With dawn came a little lull, then terrific gusts. Our tent was going, and George and I rushed into boots and parkas, and blundered out into the storm as the tent went down, its poles snapped and the fabric torn. Each pulled his sleeping bag from the wreckage and crawled into another tent. A second trip for food was all we could manage in the wind and cold. Streather and Bates pretended to be glad to have me crowd into their tent, a French model with lining which made it very cramped even for two. George piled in on Dee Molenaar and Bob Craig. The storm reached its peak. The day wore on.

Can such an ordeal be remotely conceived as "pleasure" or "sport"? Are we masochists to "enjoy" such a battering, such cold, such wind, lack of food, lack of sleep, lack of water? Emphatically not. Our stay at Camp VIII, ten days of hardship and anxiety, was terribly hard. It brought each of us down to fundamentals. The deepest springs of character were tapped for our survival. The lack of oxygen at great altitudes may dull the mind and weaken the body, but there is an inner strength of spirit, a bigger power which emerges undiminished, even magnified, to bring a man through such an experience. We faced nature's wildest forces with our pitifully feeble tents and clothing as our only weapons, plus our inner determination. Perhaps it is this conquest, conquest of one's self through survival of such an ordeal, that brings a man back to frontiers again and again. It may be a storm at sea, the arctic cold, or the desert heat. It may be a frontier of the spirit or of the mind. By testing himself beyond endurance man learns to know himself. He endures and grows. Each generation passes the limits defined by its elders: the passage of the oceans, the reaching of the poles, flight, the four-minute mile, the theory of relativity, atomic fission. In a small way the conquest of a great peak is such a frontier.

But we did not think much about *why* we had come. Our whole energies were focused on survival, though we still planned to go higher. Not one of us but wished the job were done; not one of us but longed for Base Camp and for home. Apathy grows strong on high peaks, the body becomes feeble, the force to advance declines. Simple jobs—writing a diary, taking photographs, cleaning the cooking pots—loom as major undertakings. It seems too hard, too tiring to do anything but lie still and rest, and yet someone managed to go out for more food bags, and at the same time to supply the other tents. Someone tightened the guy ropes on all tents. When we could melt snow, someone had strength to clean and fill the pots, and someone else took tea to those in the other tents. Bob Bates read aloud to us for hours. Dee Molenaar painted. We all wrote diaries; my own was now over 200 pages long. Weakened, hungry, thirsty though we were, I was able to say truthfully to Ata over the radio on August 6, "We're fine; morale is excellent. George and Tony have slightly frosted toes, and we're all thirsty, but things look pretty good."

Ata's reply, "Radio Pakistan forecasts more wind and snow," was hard.

The sixth of August was an anniversary for me, for on that day in 1934 three of us had made the first ascent of Mount Foraker in Alaska, returning late in the night through a storm much like the present, but at an altitude little more than half our present height. Surely this date must bring good luck. But when we awoke the wind was as bad as ever, and I spent the day writing in my diary a long account of our sensations, our hopes, and our fears.

During the afternoon for the first time we discussed retreat. George Bell had two frostbitten toes which had grown worse even in his sleeping bag, and Bob Craig had ominous spots on his heels. Dee was feeling poorly. Schoening, Streather, and Gilkey seemed to be the strongest, but all of us were weaker than we had been a few days before. We could not sleep much in the noise and pounding which the wind gave; we had little to drink and only cold food to eat. Retreat seemed wise, but perhaps we could recoup at Camp VI and return when the weather cleared for a final summit try.

Was this an irrational hope at this point? Was our judgment so warped by altitude that we really believed that we could go higher? Ata says no. He says, and I am inclined to agree, that we seemed in full possession of our faculties, and that our radio discussions and decisions were sound. We now believe that we were still strong enough to make the attempt, that had the weather cleared on August 7 we could have gone much higher.

We were not to be so tested. On August 7 came the cruelest blow. The day began brighter, the clouds were higher, the wind blew less. We crawled from our tents and stumbled around camp like castaways first reaching shore. As Art Gilkey crawled out to join us, he collapsed unconscious in the snow. We rushed to him and he smiled feebly. "I'm all right, fellows; it's just my leg, that's all."

We half carried him to his tent, pulled off his clothes. As soon as I examined him, I knew with a sinking heart that real trouble had hit us.

"I've had this charley horse for a couple of days now," said Art anxiously. "I thought it would be gone by now. It's sure to clear up in another day—isn't it?" The last was added in a voice that carried no assurance. The diagnosis was all too clear. Art had developed thrombophlebitis. Blood clots had formed in the veins of his left calf, cutting off the circulation and jeopardizing his leg. Already the ankle was swollen and an angry red. Reassuring him as best I could, I wrapped both legs snugly in Ace bandages and rejoined Bates and Streather in our tent. One look at my face sobered them as I explained the situation. "What's more," I concluded, "sometimes bits of clot break off and are carried to the lungs. At sea level this embolism is often fatal, and up here—" I shrugged, not having the heart to finish.

"Whatever caused this?" asked Tony. "I never heard of such a thing. Art didn't have any sickness or injury, did he?"

"I can't tell you what caused it. It's a disease which usually hits older people, or surgical patients," I explained. "I have never heard of it in healthy young mountaineers."

Then Bob asked the question we were all thinking, "How soon will he get better, Charlie? What are his chances?"

This was hard to answer. Under ideal circumstances the condition often clears in ten days to three weeks, though it may last longer. Under our conditions of dehydration, cold, and anxiety, it seemed unlikely he would improve. I didn't have the heart to add the latter, but optimistically I predicted ten days, and I explained to them the possibility of a pulmonary embolism. Bob went out to tell the other men. I sat for a few minutes, then crawled to Art's tent. I did the best I could to explain his condition, leaving out the complications, taking as optimistic a note as I could, trying to hide my awful certainty that he would never reach Base Camp alive.

By this catastrophe our whole fortunes had been changed. Before, we had been clinging to our camp, hoping for the clear weather which might bring success. Now we could only hope for weather good enough to try to lower Art down the mountain. I talked with Schoening and Craig, both of whom had done a great deal of mountain rescue work. Both said we could somehow manage to get Art down, but their statements lacked conviction. I did not believe them. I knew, we all knew, that no one could be carried, lowered, or dragged down the Black Pyramid, over the dreadful loose rock to Camp V, down House's Chimney. My mind's eye flew over the whole route. There was no hope, absolutely none. Art was crippled. He would not recover enough to walk down. We could not carry him down.

But we could try, and we must. The day seemed settled, though cloudy and cold. We packed quickly, taking sleepers, camera, food, and only one tent because Camp VI was adequately stocked. Art Gilkey, in his sleeping bag, was wrapped in the wrecked tent, and a climbing rope secured about him. In the sickly sun we took some pictures of the party. The Third American Karakoram Expedition at its highest point! About ten o'clock, with a last look around, we started off.

Just then we came close to an action which would have been fatal. I have what amounts to an obsession about leaving tidy campsites, and I hated to leave, even here, such a messy camp. So I began to throw over the cliff all of the surplus food and to pull down the tents. Someone stopped me. "Come on," he said. "The snow and wind will take care of all this mess." We started down. At first it took all our strength to pull Art through the powdery snow, waist deep. Soon, as the slope grew steeper, we had to hold back, and hold back hard. Within a few hundred yards, what we should have anticipated became obvious: the whole slope of fresh snow was ready to avalanche. New snow had piled in even deeper on the ice, snow so cold that no consolidation could occur. As we cut down this slope, jarring it, the whole mass, tons upon tons of powder snow, would have plunged down the cliff. We had watched hundreds of these powder-snow avalanches from below. Now we were too close to one. Thanks to Pete Schoening and George Bell, we saw the danger in time and started back.

Our return to camp was terribly difficult. We could neither carry nor drag Art; instead we hauled on the ropes and on his arms as he gave great leaps with his good leg. It must have been harder for him than for us, and we were close to exhaustion when we reached our tents, those tents and that food which I had come so close to casting over the cliff.

Our position, bad enough before this discovery, was now desperate. There seemed to be no real hope that Art would recover enough to climb down or even to help us lower him. We could not ourselves survive much longer under these conditions at this altitude. Already we had lived longer than any other climbers at such a high camp, and the privation and strain had taken its toll. But our escape route was cut off. It would take many days—if no new snow fell—for the slope to consolidate. I could see no hope, no way out of our position.

"Charlie, Pete and I think we can find a route down the rock ridge to the east of the ice slope. You know, on the left as you look up from Camp VII. Remember that rock ridge?" Bob Craig broke in upon my thoughts, trying to sound hopeful. "We want to have a look at it."

"Yes, I remember the ridge," I answered. "It's terribly steep; it's plastered with new snow; but it certainly will be safe from avalanches. It will be easier to lower Art down that than to drag him through the snow, and safer. Go ahead if you feel like it today."

Despite the wind and clouds, now returned in almost full force, Schoening and Craig set out. Some two hours later, while the rest of us settled in our tents, their weary shouts reported success and they straggled back to camp. Despite the wind, they had gone down the rock rim for 400 feet, and through the blown snow and driven mist had looked down and across to the ledge at Camp VII. Their route, though difficult and dangerous, was safe from avalanches. They were convinced that the unknown section between them and Camp VII could be done. At any rate, it was a way down, and it was free from avalanches.

I slept that night the sleep of utter exhaustion. Mind and body were beaten and numb. As I lay in the hazy half-light between sleep and wakening next morning, I was conscious that the wind had slackened. "This may be our chance to get Art down," I thought again and again in the dull repetition of fatigue. For an hour I lay thinking; then the stirring beside me showed that Bates and Streather too were awake, and we started breakfast.

So simple a phrase does not do justice to the complex operation involved. I lay in a narrow hole between Bob and Tony, who had the outside berths. We had changed places each day, for the two men on the outside got colder and wetter, while the middle man slept poorly on the crack between the two air mattresses and was pummeled by his neighbors on two sides instead of one. As middle man it was now my job to make tea. I twisted and crawled and wriggled, dragged a dirty pot from beneath someone's boots, filled it with snow drifted into the tent. Balancing the stove on a pot lid between my two inert companions, I was able to light it after only six matches. The *dekshi* of snow was carefully placed on top after I had wiped dry the bottom of the pot, for drips of excess snow would put out the stove. For nearly an hour I balanced the stove and dekshi till tea was made, protecting it from the flapping tent, which blew out the tiny flame several times. Finally the water boiled. Some water went to another pot for cereal, but most was for tea. Prospects of food aroused my stuporous neighbors, and in a very complex series of maneuvers they sat up and we ate. We had had so little to drink the preceding week that this meal tasted delicious and raised our spirits.

"This looks to be a good day—maybe the beginning of the good weather," said Tony.

"If it is, then we've got to decide what to do," Bob answered. "Start down with Art or wait another day or two. Do you think his leg will be well enough for him to climb down soon, Charlie?"

Sadly I destroyed this optimistic thought: "I don't think there's a chance of his climbing today or for the next week or so. We must choose between carrying him down in this dubious weather today or waiting until tomorrow in hopes it will be better."

We talked this over among ourselves for a while; then I crawled to the other tents. In each I found cheerful faces.

"Charlie," said Bob Craig, "what about a dash for the summit from here? We could do it easily."

"Or maybe we could move two men up to IX today," chimed in Pete. "I'm game. We might as well do something while we wait for Art's leg to get better."

I looked at them closely to be sure they were in earnest. Here was no foolish, blind bravado, no desperate "summit or die" attitude. Nor was there any idea of retreat without our friend. Their courage was tremendous, their morale superb.

"It seems to me we can do one of three things," I said seriously. "We can sit tight today, hoping tomorrow will be better. Carrying Art will be bad enough, and we shouldn't try it except in reasonably good weather. Or we can start for VII now, even in the clouds, because tomorrow may be bad again. The forecast just now said clouds and wind. Or, and I think this is the best idea, all of you fellows can hurry down to VI today, leaving me to take care of Art. The supplies up here will last the two of us for at least ten days, and you can all come up to help us down, well rested, when the weather is really settled."

The others were reluctant to split the party at this point, and after some discussion we decided to wait another day. Then we would either all go down or, if necessary, Streather, Art, and I would remain at VIII while the others descended.

Art felt and looked better, and his leg hurt less. "I'll be climbing again tomorrow," he said. It was heart-rending to see his courage, to know that his hope could not possibly come true. But I did hope a better day would come for the terrible work ahead of us, a day when we could see, a day without storm.

Meantime the wind decreased somewhat and the sun's heat could almost be felt through the dense cloud which enveloped us like cotton. We staggered around camp in the deep drifts, locating supplies, repitching tents. I made my daily medical rounds, looking at George's toes, which were by now badly frosted, and at Bob Craig's red and painful heels. For a long time I talked with Art, rebandaging his legs. He did seem better, but now the right leg was slightly tender, too. It was clear that he would not climb.

For several days we had talked about moving *up*. We did not want to retreat with bowed heads, beaten, discouraged. We would go down with colors flying. One last puny gesture of defiance must be made. Schoening and Craig were our fittest climbers now. They put on their warmest clothing, tied on their climbing rope, and set out—upward. For an hour they climbed through the steep new snow, over hummocks and across wide cracks. They could see nothing in the dense clouds but they were going *up*. After two hours they returned, having climbed perhaps 400 feet. They were still far from the summit cone. But their gesture underlined our spirit. We were not beaten.

At six o'clock I called Ata. "Hello, Base Camp. Hello, Base Camp. This is Camp VIII. How do you hear me?"

Cheerful as always, Ata replied, "I hear you very well, Charlie. How is Art? How are you all standing up in this storm?"

"We are very good, Ata," I tried to sound sure. "Art seems a little better today, but I don't see any prospect of his being able to climb for a long time." I went on, "What have you to suggest for therapy, Ata?"

"Charlie, that isn't my field," said Ata, an eye specialist. "I can't suggest anything to do for him but what you're already doing. But I do strongly urge that I come up to help you. After all, you have two or three frostbite cases besides Art, and I can share your burden. Over."

My eyes watered at this new sign of this wonderful man's affection for us, his determination to share our ordeal. "Ata," I replied, "you can't possibly get up here in this weather."

"I could try," he broke in.

"And furthermore," I went on, "there isn't anything you can do. We must handle this from here."

I talked over our plans with him and he agreed with our decision: if the next day were not good enough to carry Art down, the others would proceed to VI, leaving me with Art and Tony, who insisted on staying with us.

"Pray for good weather, Ata," I concluded.

"You are fighting now for all your lives," said Ata. "We here in Base Camp have been praying for you for many days."

August 9 was grim and cold. The storm returned in all its fury. Snow screamed against the tent; wind beat upon us in renewed viciousness. Nothing could be done. We could not leave the tents and live.

This was our lowest time. For the first time I thought we might all perish here in this pitiless storm. We would never leave Art; none of us had even thought of it. But we could not move him in storm; indeed, we could not move ourselves in the storm of that day.

Art had begun to cough during the night, a dry, hacking cough. My fears were confirmed as I listened to his chest. At least two clots had been carried to his lungs, for I could hear two congested areas. He looked dreadful; his pulse was pounding at 140 per minute. But his courage never faltered. He had no pain—he said—but he admitted that the cough was a nuisance. I moved in with him that morning and Schoening took my place. Through the stormy afternoon we talked briefly or read. There was little to say. We knew the odds against us, but we had made our plans. Art said nothing of himself. He had never talked about his death, though he was too wise not to see its imminence. He apologized for being a burden upon us. He encouraged us, spoke of another summit attempt—after we got him down.

The embolism to his lungs made retreat even more imperative. He could not live long up here. He would probably not live through the descent, but we must give him all the chance we could. We must do it soon. That evening I called Base Camp. "Ata, Art has had a pulmonary embolism. His condition is poor. We *must* get him off the mountain. We are going to start down tomorrow unless the weather is impossible. All of us are weaker, but morale is very high. I will call you tomorrow morning at seven. If possible we'll start soon afterward."

On that note we slept.

We all knew now that some of us might never get down the mountain alive. Each had long recognized the near impossibility of evacuating an injured man from the upper ledges of K2. We had told one another that "if somebody broke a leg, you never could get him down the mountain," but now that we were faced with Gilkey's helplessness, we realized that we *had* to get him down. We didn't know how, but we knew that we had to do it.

Schoening in particular, and also Bob Craig and Dee Molenaar, had done a lot of mountain rescue work, and the rest of us placed great confidence in their faith that somehow we could get our casualty to Base Camp. Gilkey's high morale and his confidence in us was a great boost to our spirits and we faced the job ahead with strong determination. When on the morning of August 10 Charlie Houston thrust his shoulders through the tunnel entrance of the tent where Schoening, Streather, and I, shoulder rubbing shoulder, had tossed during the long night hours, we spoke almost in unison: "How is he?"

"We've got to take him down," said the doctor. "His other leg has a clot now and he can't last long here."

The wind was hammering the tent fabric so hard that we had to yell at one another. Drifts of fine powder snow were sifting in through a strained seam in the tent vestibule, though we had done our best to keep the shelter airtight, and we could feel the whole tent vibrate as gusts stretched the fabric to the utmost.

"What? Move in this storm?" said someone.

"We've got to," said Houston. "He'll soon be dead if we don't get him down."

Nothing needed saying after that, for we knew what this decision meant. All of us had fought mountain storms before, but we had never seen anything like the duration and violence of this furious wind and snow that was still battering us. We all knew the story of the storm on Nanga Parbat in 1934, when nine members of a German expedition had died of exhaustion while battling the wind and snow. Willy Merkl, Uli Wieland, and Willi Welzenbach had been famous mountaineers, but a storm had exhausted them and killed them one by one. Here on K2 we had not only the storm to fight but the steepest part of the mountain, and we were trying to bring down these precipitous slopes a crippled companion as well!

We all realized that our adventure had now become grim, for the odds against getting Art down were obvious, and our own position was getting more critical all the time. While Houston and Schoening were easing Art out of his tent into the storm, the rest of us began packing light loads to take down. We would need one tent in case of emergency, and we took the Gerry tent, our lightest one. We also might need a stove and pot, and some meat bars, chocolate, or quick-energy food that needed no cooking. Often the effects of altitude so weaken one's determination that doing nothing becomes a positive pleasure, but this was no time for lethargy, and as we moved purposefully out of the tents into the stinging blasts of snow, we knew that we had to move fast, while fingers and toes still had feeling. Little was spoken. Each of us realized that he was beginning the most dangerous day's work of his lifetime.

Gilkey seemed in no pain as we wrapped him in the smashed tent, put his feet in a rucksack, and tied nylon ropes to him in such a way that they cradled him. Four ropes, tied to this cradle, could be held by one man ahead, one man behind, and one on either side. We had already put on all our warm clothing—

sweaters, wool jackets, down jackets, and nylon parkas—and stripped our packs to the minimum. As we worked, the disabled man watched the preparations silently. He was an experienced mountaineer and realized what all of us were up against. But he knew also that we would never leave him, and that we would bring him down safely if it were humanly possible. Art's cap was pulled down over his face, which looked drawn and bluish-gray, but he gave a wan smile whenever someone asked, "How is it going?"

"Just fine," he would say. "Just fine." And his mouth would smile. He never showed a moment's fear or the slightest lack of confidence, but he realized of course that he had been stricken by something that was likely to be fatal, that his condition was getting worse, and that he was 9,000 feet above Base Camp in a terrible monsoon storm. The nearest tent, at Camp VI, was 2,000 feet below. He knew that we could not carry him down the tricky route we had come up, and that we must go only where we could lower him. Even in perfect weather with all men in top physical condition, the task might prove impossible—yet Art Gilkey could smile, and his smile gave us strength.

While we were adjusting the tow ropes, Schoening and Molenaar strapped on their crampons and disappeared into the storm. They were to find the best route past the dangerous avalanche slope that had blocked us a few days before, and to go over to the Camp VII cache to get a climbing rope that was strung on the ice slope just above. It would be useful in the descent. After their departure Houston called Base Camp on the walkie-talkie and told Ata-Ullah our plans. "It's pretty desperate, Ata," he said grimly, "but we can't wait. We're starting down now. We'll call you at three o'clock."

Each man took his place on a rope tied to Gilkey and for a couple of hundred yards we lunged hard at the tow ropes to pull Art through the knee-deep drifts of powder snow; then gravity took over and we had to hold back just as strongly to keep our helpless 185-pound load from plunging into the abyss. The steep slope we were on disappeared below us into nothingness. Was there a cliff there, a jumping-off place? We strained our eyes peering into the storm, but we could not wait for clearing weather. Instead we had to depend on Schoening and Molenaar, who had gone ahead to scout out the way. As we descended, Craig and Bell pulled the front ropes, one on each side, and Houston directed operations from a point immediately behind Gilkey, while Streather and I anchored the rope higher up. Gradually we worked our way to a rock ridge, climbed down alongside it, and then began to lower Gilkey down a steep snow slope leading to a snow chute and an ice gully below. This route was not the one we would have taken had Gilkey been able to walk, but now we had no choice: we could go only where we could lower our companion, and we had faith that the two men ahead would find a route down. Once we were well started, return to Camp VIII would be impossible for any of us.

The wind and cold seeped insidiously through our layers of warm clothing so that by the end of the third hour none of us had feeling in his toes any longer, and grotesque icicles hung from our eyebrows, beards, and mustaches. Goggles froze over and we continually raised them on our foreheads in order to see how to handle the rope. Moving the sick man was frightfully slow. We had to belay one another as well as Gilkey, and our numb fingers would not move quickly. Somehow, when we got to the steepest pitch, however, someone managed to tie two 120-foot nylon ropes together and we started to lower Gilkey down, down in the only direction the slope would permit. Houston and I, braced on the storm-swept ridge, backs to the wind, could feel the terrible gusts trying to hurl us off the rocks. We could not see where we were lowering Art, but we could hear faint shouts from Schoening and Molenaar, who were out of sight below. As we slowly payed out the coils of rope, thankful that they were of nylon and would not freeze in kinks, Bob Craig unroped from us and climbed down alongside the injured man to direct the descent. Soon he was completely obscured, too, but Streather climbed down to where he could see Craig's arm signals, yet still see us, and so we belayers had communication with Craig and Gilkey and knew whether to lower or to hold the rope. Alternately we anchored and payed out line until we were nearly frozen, and our arms were strained when Tony Streather, whom we could barely see, turned and shouted, "Hold tight! They're being carried down in an avalanche!"

We held. Our anchorage was good and the rope stretched taut. For a moment snow flurries blotted out everything, and then we could hear a muffled shout from Streather. "They're still there!" The rope had broken loose a wind-slab avalanche of powder snow that had roared down over both men, blotting them from sight. Craig clung to the rope to Gilkey, and held on to it for his life. The pull of the hissing particles must have been terrible, but the avalanche was of unconsolidated snow. The falling powder slithered out of sight and down off the side of the mountain, where it must have kept falling long after we could hear it. When it was gone, Craig still clung to the rope, gray and very chilled. Both men were safe. The grim descent continued.

Schoening and Molenaar, who were not far from Camp VII, soon were able to reach Gilkey, but it seemed like hours to the four of us on the icy rocks of the wind-swept ridge before they shouted up that they had him strongly belayed "on the edge of a cliff," and we could climb down. Stiffly we shifted from our frozen positions, and climbed clumsily down the steep, crumbly rocks to the snow chute above the ice gully. Houston and I were on one rope, Bell and Streather on the other. All were so cold, so near exhaustion, that moving down over dangerous, snow-covered ice stretched us to the limit. Through the murk of blowing snow we saw Schoening standing in front of a large, rounded rock that had become frozen onto a narrow ledge. His ice ax was thrust deep into the snow above the rock, and the rope with which he held Art Gilkey was looped tightly around the shaft of the ax. The sick man was at the edge of a 20-foot cliff, beneath which we could glimpse the ice gully dropping off steeply into the storm toward the Godwin-Austen Glacier nearly

2 miles below.

Schoening looked like a man from another world. So much frost had formed on our beards that faces were unrecognizable, and we knew that we were fast reaching the breaking point. We could not continue much longer without shelter from the driving storm and food to renew our energy. Some 150 yards below us to the east was the tiny shelf, nicked into the ice slope, where Schoening and Gilkey had spent the night of July 30 during their reconnaissance above Camp VI. We had called it Camp VII, or Camp VII cache. None of us had expected anyone to spend another night there, but Bob Craig, whose struggle against the avalanche had so completely exhausted him temporarily that he could hardly tie a crampon strap, had been belayed over to this site to rest and clear some of the avalanche snow that had seeped under his parka. We yelled to him to try to enlarge the ledge. Meanwhile, with Schoening anchoring the rope, we lowered Gilkey slowly over the short rock cliff until he was resting against the 45-degree ice slope. Streather, who was roped to Bell, climbed down to Gilkey. Schoening held Gilkey's rope firmly while Houston belayed me across a delicate pitch of steep, hard ice, and then Houston climbed down to a point opposite the man suspended against the slope. The problem now was not to get Gilkey down, but to swing him across the steep ice slope to the ice shelf at Camp VII. Our plan was to get a firm anchorage and then pendulum him across, but unfortunately the ice near him was too hard for axes to be driven in and the slope was relentlessly steep.

Even during the best weather conditions the maneuver would have been dangerous, and our position at that moment I shall never forget. Schoening was belaying Gilkey, who hung 60 feet below him, suspended against the sharply angled ice. On the same level as Gilkey, and 40 feet across from him, five of us, facing into the stinging, drifting snow, were searching for a place where we could stand and anchor the rope to Gilkey as we pulled him across the ice in the direction of Craig on the ice shelf. With our spiked crampons biting the hard ice, Streather,

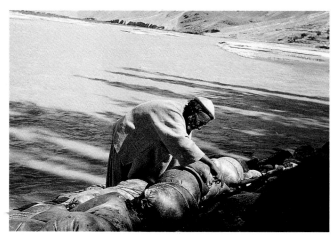

Throughout Baltistan, rivers are major barriers to travel. By carefully skinning goats, tying off neck and legs, the skin can be inflated and, with a framework of tough willow branches, can make an unsinkable, if frightening, raft.

Rope bridges are made of woven vines and branches, and until the recent construction of proper wire rope suspension bridges, were maintained by villagers on each side of the river. They tended to turn over in a high wind, and the side rails had to be held apart by a man stationed in the middle, over whom one had to climb.

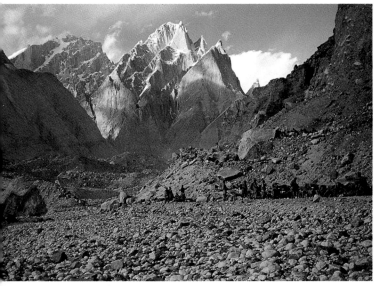

We were awed by the size and grandeur of the immense walls along the Baltoro – some of the great rock faces in the world.

Seen from the Baltoro, Masherbrum is a spectacular and challenging mountain, attempted in 1938 and finally climbed in 1956 by a party led by Nick Clinch, which included George Bell.

Paiju rises above the terminus of the Baltoro Glacier like some magnificent Gothic cathedral, brilliantly lighted here by the rising sun.

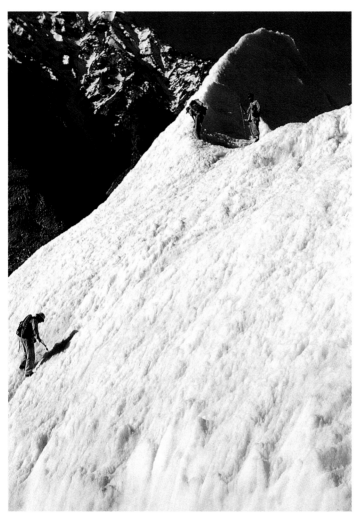

The ice "ships" of the Baltoro are giant ice towers seemingly thrust up from the ice below. They are found on few other glaciers and exactly how they are formed is not understood. Nowhere are they so high and large.

Seen from Urdokass, the Mustagh Tower, though impressive, is not as sheer as it appears in the well-known photograph by Sella.

This is how K2 looks on a clear day to those ascending the Godwin-Austen Glacier from Concordia. The Angelus is on the left.

Though the view of K2 from Concordia is sometimes dramatic, the march up to its 16,000-foot base is exhausting.

Among the best porters in the Karakoram, these men came from Satpura, a village twenty miles from Skardu. They were especially helpful on our return from the mountain.

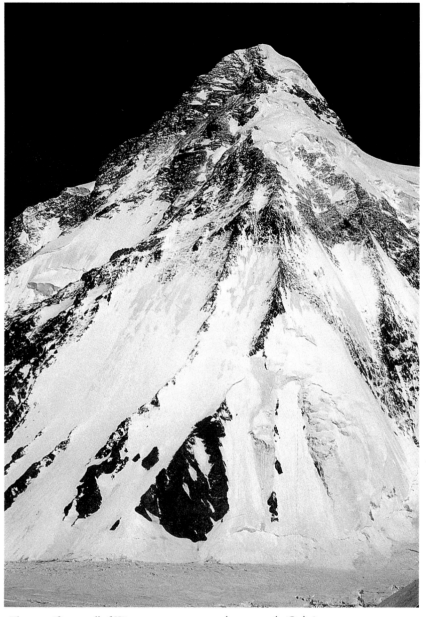

The magnificent wall of K2 seems to grow as one advances up the Godwin-Austen Glacier towards Windy Gap.

Looking up 12,000 feet from our base camp, one had difficulty estimating the scale, the steepness and the complexity of the southern face, a series of rock and ice cliffs.

From our base camp we walked five miles, climbing 1500 feet up the glacier over deep crevasses and sharp ridges of tortured ice to reach Camp I.

Bob Bates had developed an abcessed tooth at Camp II and Houston did his first extraction before an admiring crowd.

K2 is unrelentingly steep and always spectacular, especially up to Camp III where the climbing is not so technically difficult as it becomes higher on the mountain.

Tents must be placed wherever a narrow ledge can be scraped or built up on the steep Abruzzi Ridge. The 'siege tactics' used in early Himalayan climbs required placement of many more camps than is customary today.

About the only nearly-level area on the whole Abruzzi Ridge is the snow shoulder at about 25,000 feet, where there is ample room for tents, but where the wind, howling from across the shoulder, held us hostage for ten days.

Above Camp V, the route runs up the formidable Black Pyramid, so called because of its shape and color as seen from across the valley. The rock is very steep, smoothed by wind and falls of rock and ice. The route is difficult and dangerous.

*During our first day or two at Camp VIII, occasional breaks
in the clouds allowed Dee Molenaar to create this sketch of the panorama
one might see through a 100-degree arc from high on the mountain.*

Based on photographs taken by others and his projection of the right half of the peak from ground-level views, Dee Molenaar painted the southern face of K-2 as seen from Broad Peak across the upper Godwin-Austin Glacier.

Badly battered and shaken, we had a sad memorial service for Art Gilkey at a great cairn built by the porters above the Base Camp.

The Accident

© D. MOLENAAR 1994

Houston, Molenaar, and I stood close together. Bell and Streather were roped together, Houston and I were on a rope together—and Molenaar had just "tied in" to a loose rope to Gilkey. He had done this when Craig had unroped and gone over to the ice shelf to rest, and it was Molenaar's precaution that saved us all. For George Bell, who was some 60 feet above us, began to descend a delicate stretch of hard ice in order to help with Gilkey's ropes. At that moment, what we had all been dreading occurred. Something threw Bell off balance and he fell.

I never saw Bell fall, but to my horror I saw Streather being dragged off the slope and making desperate efforts to jam the pick of his ax into the ice and stop. Streather had been standing above the rope from Houston to me. In almost the same instant I saw Houston swept off, and though I turned and lunged at the hard ice with the point of my ax, a terrible jerk ripped me from my hold and threw me backward headfirst down the slope. *This is it!* I thought as I landed heavily on my pack. There was nothing I could do now. We had done our best, but our best wasn't good enough. This was the end. Since nobody was on the rope with Houston and me, there was no one else to hold us, and I knew that nothing could stop us now. On the slope below, no rock jutted on which the rope between us could catch. Only thousands of feet of empty space separated us from the glacier below. It was like falling off a slanting Empire State Building six times as high as the real one.

Thrown violently backward, with the hood of my down jacket jammed over my eyes, I had a feeling of unreality, of detachment. The future was beyond my control. All I knew was that I landed on my pack with great force, bouncing faster and faster, bumping over rocks in great thumps. The next bound I expected to take me over a cliff in a terrible drop that would finish it all, when, by a miracle, I stopped sliding.

I was on my back with my hood over my eyes and my head a yard below my feet. My arms, stretched over my head, were so completely tangled with the taut rope that I could not loosen them. I was helpless, and when I tried to move, I realized that I was balanced on the crest of some rocks and that a change of position might throw me off the edge. The rope had apparently snagged on a projection—though how and where I couldn't imagine—but it might not be securely caught. Whether it was firmly held, whether anyone else was alive, I did not know, but I didn't need to wait. Almost immediately I heard a groan coming from nearly on top of me. "Get me loose," I called, and immediately I felt the pressure of a leg braced against my shoulder and the rope was pulled off my arms.

Grabbing a rock, I swung my head around. Dee Molenaar

and I were clinging to a rocky outcrop at the side of a steep ice
slope, studded with rocks, about 150 to 200 feet below the place
where we had been working on the ropes to Gilkey. Blood from
Dee's nose trickled across his mustache and beard, and he
looked badly shaken. My rope was tight to someone or something above, and I heard a distant yell, "Get your weight off the
rope!" Fifty feet higher, through a mist of blowing snow, I could
see Tony Streather staggering to his feet, a tangle of ropes still
tight about his waist. Below me I heard a cry, "My hands are
freezing!" and, looking down, to my amazement I saw George
Bell, who seconds before had been 60 feet above me. Now about
60 feet *below,* he was climbing up over the edge of nothingness.
He wore neither pack nor glasses and was staggering up over
the steep rocks, obviously dazed, with his hands held out gro-
tesquely in front of him. His mittens had been ripped off in the
fall, and already the color of his hands had turned an ugly
fish-belly white. If his hands were badly frozen, of course, we
might never be able to get him down off the mountain.

Turning to Molenaar, I thrust my pack into his arms. Most
of the lashing had ripped loose and the walkie-talkie radio,
which had been on top, was gone; my sleeping bag was half off,
held by a single twist of line. Without sleeping bags we were
unlikely to survive the night, no matter how we tried! Since
Molenaar wore no pack, I imagined that his sleeping bag also
had been torn off in the fall. Whether or not the tent someone
had been carrying had survived the fall, I didn't know. "For
God's sake, hold this," I yelled above the wind, placing my load
in Molenaar's arms. (For all I knew, mine was the only sleeping
bag to survive the fall, and we must not lose it now.) The loose
pack was awkward to hold securely while we were standing on
such steep rock, but Molenaar grasped it and I unroped and
started to climb shakily down to meet Bell. As I climbed down,
I wondered about the ropes that had saved us. They were
snagged to something up above, but the driving snow kept us
from seeing what was holding them. Luckily I had a spare pair
of dry, loosely woven Indian mitts in the pouch pocket of my

parka, and when I reached Bell, whose face was gray and haggard, I helped him to put them on. Already his fingers were so stiff with cold that he couldn't move them, but balancing on projections of rock on the steep slope, we struggled to save his hands and finally forced the big white mittens past his stiff thumbs and down over his wrists.

Bell's fall had ended with him suspended over the edge of a ledge, below which the slope dropped away precipitously for thousands of feet. The weight of his pack pulled him head down, and he had lost it while trying to get right side up and back over the ledge. While Bell crouched down, working desperately to warm his hands under his parka, I left him, for Molenaar and I had seen a crumpled figure lying below a 30-foot cliff on a narrow shelf that seemed projecting over utter blankness below. It was Houston. Somehow a rope to him was snagged high above us, too. Climbing unsteadily but cautiously, for I was not roped and felt shaken by the fall, I worked my way down the steep rocks and across to the ledge. Houston was unconscious, but his eyes opened as I touched his shoulder. When he staggered to his feet, I felt relief it is impossible to describe.

"Where are we?" he asked. "What are we doing here?"

He was obviously hurt. His eyes did not focus and he appeared to be suffering from a concussion. Again and again I tried to persuade him to climb up the cliff, while Molenaar anchored the rope still attached to him from above. He didn't understand. "Where are we?" he kept saying, for my replies did not convey any meaning to him in his confused state.

The wind and blowing snow were searing our faces. We were all near exhaustion and in danger of crippling frostbite. If we were to survive, we had to get shelter at once, or we would be so numbed by exposure that we could not protect ourselves. What had happened in that Nanga Parbat storm which had taken so many men was a grim reminder. All of us working together did not now have strength enough to pull or carry Houston up the steep rock and snow to the ice ledge, 150 feet above, which we had called Camp VII.

"Charlie," I said with the greatest intensity, looking directly into his eyes, "if you ever want to see Dorcas and Penny again [his wife and daughter], climb up there right *now!*"

Somehow this demand penetrated to his brain, for, with a frightened look and without a word, he turned and, belayed by Molenaar, fairly swarmed up the snowy rocks of the cliff. Instinct and years of climbing helped him now in his confused condition, for he climbed brilliantly up to Molenaar. I followed more slowly because, being fully conscious, I had great respect for this steep rock wall, and with great care I pulled myself up over the snow-covered slabs. When I reached Molenaar, he was looking puzzled and very unhappy as he tried to answer Houston's repeated question, "What are we doing here?"

10 *The Bivouac*

ROBERT H. BATES

When I reached Molenaar, I still did not know what had caused the near disaster or how all five of us who fell had been saved. Up above, through the murk of blinding snow, I caught glimpses of Art Gilkey, anchored where he had been before the fall, but now Bob Craig was near him. Tony Streather, in a direct line above me, seemed to be untangling himself from a confused snarl of nylon climbing ropes, one of which led down to me.

Much later I learned the sequence of events that had put us in this position and marveled even more at our escape. When Bell fell, he pulled off Streather, who was hurled into the rope between Houston and me and became tangled with it. We were in turn knocked off by the impact, and all three of us—Streather, Houston, and I—began tumbling in a blind, uncontrolled whirl toward the glacier far below. Nothing we could do could stop us now. But our time had not come. For Molenaar was standing below us on the slope, farther away from the sick man, and he had just tied one of the loose ropes from Art Gilkey about his waist. That circumstance saved us, for our wild fall sent us all into and across the rope from Gilkey to Molenaar, and somehow Streather fouled onto this rope too. But our impact had thrown Molenaar headfirst down the slope, and we all bounded on unchecked until stopped by the tightening of the rope from Gilkey to Molenaar—a rope in which Streather was now completely tangled. Gilkey was not pulled loose, for he was anchored by Schoening, who stood on a rock ledge 60 feet above him, and the whole strain of the five falling men, plus Gilkey, was transmitted to Schoening, the youngest member of the party. Fortunately for us all, Schoening is an expert belayer, and his skill and quick thinking saved our lives. Later he told us how he did it.

By the time I returned to Molenaar and Houston, it was clear that through some miracle every climber was still able to move under his own power, but our exposure to the wind-driven snow was chilling us dangerously; we had to move fast to take shelter before we became too numb to set up a tent or became so crippled by frostbite that we would never be able to continue the descent. Since Molenaar's leg hurt and he didn't feel like moving much, I took Charlie Houston's rope and began climbing slowly up toward the ice ledge at Camp VII. I couldn't hurry, to save my life. Houston was obviously confused, but by instinct he climbed well and did what was asked. I hadn't climbed far when Tony Streather threw me a rope-end, and then Bob Craig returned from anchoring Art Gilkey and he and Streather took over the task of escorting Houston to the ledge. Craig had not seen the fall, but had looked up suddenly and been horrified to see the slope bare except for Schoening and Gilkey and a solitary ice ax with its pick end jabbed into the ice. At that moment a cloud of snow had blown across the ice, blotting out everything. When it cleared, Schoening, whose tight grip on the rope was freezing his hands, called to Craig to help him to anchor Gilkey. The sick man had not fallen, and he lay suspended against the ice as he had been at the time of the accident. He was probably the warmest of us all, but we could not continue to move him until the injured were cared for and we had more manpower to help get him across the slope.

When Craig reached him, Art handed over his ice ax, which he had retained for use in the descent. To make a secure anchorage was not easy, and Craig, still exhausted from his struggle against the avalanche, was not secured by anyone while he did it, but he skillfully found firm snow and drove in Art's ice ax right up to the head. He told the sick man that we would return for him as soon as we had a tent up. Gilkey understood. Not until then, when Craig had an ice ax firmly embedded, could Pete Schoening release his grip—which had held six men!—and begin to warm his freezing hands. Craig had not been involved in the accident, but all the rest of us owed our lives to Schoening's skill, courage, and technique.

Fortunately the tent had not been in one of the lost packs, but as I started to unroll it, the wind threatened to sweep it off the mountain. Craig and I were trying to wrestle the corners of the tent into position when Streather, who had now anchored Gilkey with a second ice ax, joined us to help pin the flapping edges under loose rocks till we could get anchorage for the guy ropes. The slope was so steep that the outer third of the tent was off the ledge and overhanging, so that it was impossible to keep the wind from sucking under the tent and trying to tear it away.

We were fortunate that this was our smallest two-man tent, for it held the ledge better than a wider one. Actually, in Exeter before the expedition, we had thought it too small for two men and had almost failed to bring it. Pitching the tent was frustrating, for each time we would secure one corner, another corner would shudder loose. Finally we tied the front guy rope to a rock piton and lashed the inside corners as well as we could to projecting rocks. When Bob Craig later pounded in a Bernays ice piton, we felt somewhat safer, though the nylon shroud line attached to it didn't look too strong and the outer section of the tent bulged out over the slope. If someone inside forgot how precariously the tent was poised and leaned against the outer wall, we knew that the fabric would probably tear or the whole tent pull loose from the little ledge, and with everyone in it roll down the mountain into space.

The moment the tent was up, we moved Bell and Houston inside, where they would be under shelter and their weight would be useful in anchoring the tent. Molenaar at this point joined them to help take care of Houston, for Dee by now had lashed my loose pack together and carried it to the ledge. His left thigh hurt and he had a cracked rib.

While these men were trying to warm themselves in the tent, the rest of us began to hack out another platform in the ice for Schoening's bivouac tent, which had previously been cached on the ledge as a safeguard for Streather and me on the day when we climbed from Camp VI to Camp VIII. This tent was meant for one person or in an emergency two, but if we could get it up, we meant to use it for three men to huddle inside.

At this moment Peter Schoening climbed down to us and declared laconically, "My hands are freezing." He too crawled into the tent to try to save his hands. All of us were still too busy to find out how Schoening had held us, for it seemed as if we would never get a platform flat enough or wide enough to pitch the bivouac tent. All our strength and energy went into chipping out an ice platform, for we had to get shelter from the bitter blast for everyone; but when we did get an uneven floor carved out, the wind whipped the fabric violently. It was like working in the slipstream behind an airplane as it taxied across the snow, spraying stinging particles behind. Finally Pete crawled out to help us insert the poles and we fastened the tent insecurely to rocks and pitons near the shelf of ice. It too overhung in an alarming manner.

The moment the bivouac tent was up, three of us prepared to go back for Art Gilkey. He was only 150 feet away, but a low rib of rock hid from sight the ice gully where we had left him suspended from the two widely separated ice axes, each firmly thrust into the snow. Gilkey had called to us a couple of times while we were desperately hacking at the slope to make a platform for the bivouac tents, but the severity of the storm and the position of the gully made it impossible to distinguish words. Gilkey sounded as if he were shouting encouragement, but the wind blurred his words, as it must have muffled our answering shouts to him. He knew that we were making a shelter and would come for him as soon as we could.

About ten minutes after Gilkey's last shout, Streather, Craig, and I roped up and began to cross the slope to reach the injured man and move him somehow to the ice ledge where we now had two small tents. We knew that moving him even this short distance would take every bit of strength we had left, and we roped together carefully and braced ourselves for the effort.

Schoening would have come with us, but as he emerged from the tent, he began a fit of coughing so long and painful that it doubled him up and made us urge him to crawl back into the tent. Pete had gulped in deep draughts of frigid air while climbing up to collect the fixed rope above Camp VII earlier in the day, and apparently the cold had somehow temporarily affected his lungs. He coughed until he seemed exhausted. At the moment we were particularly dismayed by Schoening's near collapse, because he had always been strong and we were counting heavily on him to help in moving Gilkey and in getting the party down the mountain. We didn't know at the moment what his trouble was or how serious it might be, and in great distress we started out into the wind to traverse the slope to Art Gilkey. Streather and I had had our snow glasses off most of the day, because snow had frozen over the lenses, turning them almost to blinders. Apparently we had developed a touch of snow blindness, because we now seemed to be seeing everything through a very light mist. This mist was hard to distinguish from blowing snow, and we seemed to be moving in a dream. Fortunately, the wind had dropped as we reached the rock rib and looked into the gully where Art had been left suspended. What we saw there I shall never forget. The whole slope was bare of life. Art Gilkey was gone!

Our sick comrade, who had called to us a few minutes before, had disappeared. Even the two ice axes used to anchor him safely had been torn loose. The white, wind-swept ice against which he had been resting showed no sign that anyone had ever been there. It was as if the hand of God had swept him away.

The shock stunned us. Blowing snow stung our faces as we silently stared and stared, but the slope remained empty. Something about it had changed, however, for there seemed to be a groove on the lower part of the slope that had not been there before. A snow or ice avalanche must have swept the sick man away scant minutes before we came to get him. As Craig and I belayed Streather out onto the center of the gully, he looked down past his cramponed feet to where the slope disappeared into the storm below. We called and shouted, but all of us knew that there would be no answer. Nobody could slide off that slope out of sight and remain alive. Dazed and incredulous, we turned and plodded back to the tents.

Gilkey's death, though anticipated for other reasons, was a violent shock. He had been very close to us, and we could not forget his many kindnesses to each of us in the past weeks. We had admired him and loved him. But too many immediate problems faced us to permit brooding over our loss now. Several men were injured. Whether they were in condition to climb down the mountain without help, we didn't know; nor did we know whether we could get them down if they could not walk. We would never leave anybody, but our struggle to lower Art Gilkey had shown us that to get a helpless man down the upper slopes of K2 under storm conditions required more strength and manpower than we now had. The route down from Camp VII to Camp VI would be longer and infinitely more difficult for rescue work than anything we had yet descended.

At Schoening's request, I moved into the Gerry tent alongside Houston. Four of us were now crowded into this little shelter with our backs to the ice slope and our feet resting lightly on the one-third of the tent which bellied out and overhung the slope. Luckily we had an air mattress, and once this was inflated and worked under the men inside, it gave some insulation from the cold. I opened my sleeping bag and placed the outer bag under our feet on the droopy side of the tent, while the inner half I wrapped around Houston, who was in a state of shock.

By this time the sky was darkening, but to our great relief the wind had dropped. We wore all our clothes and though they were damp we were not too cold, yet the night was a ghastly experience. George Bell, his hands and feet frozen, had jammed his great bulk into one end of the little Gerry tent. He cannot see well without glasses, and the pair he was wearing and the spare pair in his pack had disappeared in the fall. That night he must have realized the effort that would be required of him next day, for the steepest part of the route lay immediately below our ledge, and it would be impossible for us to carry him if he could not climb down. At the opposite end of the tent lay Dee Molenaar, a deep cut stiffening his left thigh and a bruised or cracked rib making his breathing painful. What he was thinking during the long hours of darkness I don't know, but he insisted on covering up Houston in his down jacket, even though he himself was lying exposed just inside the doorway of the tent.

Between Molenaar and Bell were Houston and I. Charlie Houston usually is bursting with energy, and if he had had his normal strength that night he would have been far too powerful for us. At first he was in a state of shock, but he soon stopped shivering and began to ask question after question, "Where are we?" "Where is Pete?" "How is Art?" Some things he seemed to understand, but he would ask the same questions again and again. A dozen times at least during the night he would ask, "How's Pete?" I would say, "He's all right," but Charlie wouldn't believe me. Then I would call across to the tiny bivouac tent, which was swelled to bursting by the three men inside, "Hey, Pete, tell Charlie you're all right."

Pete Schoening would call out, "I'm fine, Charlie. Don't worry about me."

"Oh, that's fine; that's fine," Charlie would say, and for a moment he would be quiet. Then again he would say solicitously, "How's Tony?" and the rigmarole would begin all over again. We were touched by his anxiety about us but we were more concerned about him.

During the fall Houston had evidently struck his forehead against a rock, causing a concussion and a hemorrhage which blurred the vision in his right eye. Another blow had given him a painful chest injury, which so affected his breathing that any deep breath was painful. In his confused state he thought that the pain in his chest when he breathed was caused by lack of oxygen in the tent, and so he tried to remedy the situation by clawing a hole in the fabric. Then, to keep from breathing deeply, he would take short breaths, faster and faster, until he would slump over unconscious and then he would breathe normally until he became conscious again. When he became unconscious, we would shift position and try to get more comfortable, for the moment he was conscious he would become active again and we would have to restrain him.

Somehow—I still don't know how—the three men crammed into the bivouac tent, which was just as precariously pitched, were able to make tea and pass it in to us occasionally. There wasn't a great deal, but those swallows of tea were a godsend. They helped us to keep awake. Molenaar even opened the tent door to humor Charlie, but he still wanted to cut a hole in the tent. "I know about these things," he would say. "I have studied them. We'll all be dead in three minutes if you won't let me cut a hole in the tent." And again his breathing would speed up tremendously and he would collapse.

The night seemed unbearably long, but at least we could converse with those in the other tent and the tea cheered us. During the long darkness we asked each man about his injuries and each man told a compressed story of what had happened to him in the fall. Schoening wasn't saying much, but we kept calling over to him, "How did you do it, Pete?"

"What kind of a belay did you have?"

"If you can stop five men at 25,000 feet, how many could you stop at 15,000?"

Pete's story was brief. "Well, I was lucky," he said. "My ice ax was driven into the snow and braced against the upper side of that big boulder frozen in the ice. The rope passed around the ax to where I stood in front of the boulder, and went around my body, so that the force was widely distributed. Of course I was belaying Art anyway, and when I saw George slip and then Tony and the others pulled off, I swung weight onto the head of the ax and held on as the rope slid a bit. The force must have come in a series of shocks. The strain on me was not too great, but at the ice ax that seven-sixteenth-inch nylon rope stretched until it looked like a quarter-inch line, and I was scared stiff the boulder would be pulled loose. If that happened, the ax, which was braced against it, would go, too, and we would be lost. For minutes, it seemed, the rope was taut as a bowstring. Snow squalls blotted out everything below, and I couldn't tell what was happening. My hands were freezing, but of course I could not let go. Then the air cleared a bit and I yelled to Bob Craig, who was over at Camp VII, to come and anchor Art. By the time he reached him, most of the weight was off the rope, and from below I could hear someone calling, 'Charlie's hurt.' Once Art was secured, I came down to thaw out."

This simple story failed to stress the remarkable fact that one man had held five men who slid 150 to 300 feet down a 45-degree slope and that he had done it at nearly 25,000 feet, where the mere job of survival absorbs most of the strength of a man. Such magnificent belay work has rarely been recorded in mountaineering anywhere. Nor have I read of any other climbing miracle when three separate ropes fouled together to save the lives of five men. Bad luck had forced us to move in storm and had placed us where the fall had swept us off, but good luck, the resilience of nylon rope, and a remarkable tangle had saved our lives.

When the long hours finally wore away and the first rays of daylight came, a dour gray sky showed that more storm was coming fast. Silent, haggard, exhausted, we waited until Bob Craig had first made some tea and then cooked a little cereal. We had only one pot. During the night someone had placed the other pot outside the door of the crowded tent and it had immediately slid off the mountain. At the first light Houston crawled to the door and thrust out his shoulders. He seemed astonished that he didn't find more oxygen or easier breathing outside the tent. The morning air was raw and we were sore and weary. Everyone's eyes looked dead. But there was no question about the next move. We had to go down.

11 *From Camp VII to Camp II*

ROBERT H. BATES

During the long hours of darkness we had had much to think about, and in the morning we soberly assessed our situation. Art Gilkey, who had camped here so cheerfully a few days before, was gone. Houston seemed physically able to climb but he was weak and still out of his head, had a chest injury, and couldn't reason. Whether he had internal injuries we didn't know. George Bell was an almost greater worry. His hands were covered with frostbite blisters and his feet were blotched with deeper frostbite. He wasn't sure that he could get his swollen feet into his boots again. In addition he could not see well without his glasses. Whether he and Houston could climb down, we didn't know, but we realized that we didn't have the manpower to carry them if they couldn't.

Schoening's chest seemed better during the night, but it was still a potential cause for worry. Fortunately, his hands, which he had nipped when he held the fall, had not suffered damage and did not give him trouble. Molenaar had a cracked rib and a cut on his thigh which would slow him down, but his morale was good and he was anxious to get started. Craig, too, looked exhausted, but the early morning light showed him to be obviously in better shape than he had been the evening before. Tony Streather, who with Craig and Schoening had been brewing tea for us all during the night, looked more himself than anyone else did.

Craig and Streather teamed up again to cook breakfast, and though we somehow didn't feel hungry, we drank the tea, forced down the thick cereal, and made Houston eat some. There would be many problems before we reached Base Camp again, but from now on it wouldn't do to look too far ahead. The essential thing was for us to get down out of avalanche danger to Camp VI. Once there, the most treacherous climbing would be behind us, we would be close to the food cache at Camp V, and even short periods of good weather would permit the descent to lower camps.

The wind was already rising when we finished breakfast and it took an effort of will to crawl out into the raw morning, stiff and sore, and begin to pull our packs together for the descent. Houston's crampons were hard to strap on, because there was no flat place for anyone to stand or for him to put his foot. And yet they must be strapped on tightly. George Bell was having similar problems. His neck was so stiff from his cramped position in the tent that he could not straighten his head, and for dreadful minutes it seemed that he could not force his swollen and frostbitten feet into his vapor-barrier rubber boots. Fortunately most rubber will stretch, and after much pulling and straining both boots went on.

Schoening and Craig wanted to take Houston down, for he was still suffering from the concussion, and we were all very worried about how he would climb. If he stopped climbing, if he decided to act independently or if he slipped, he might bring disaster to the teammates whom he would have risked anything to save. We knew that this day's descent was the most dangerous we faced. If we could get the whole party down to Camp VI, there was a good chance that we would all get safely off the mountain. Accordingly, when everyone's crampons were on, Houston was tied carefully into the middle of Craig's and Schoening's rope and they started to climb carefully down over the snow-covered slabs. Schoening, whose ability at belaying had been established for all time, went last and anchored the rope. Those of us who were to follow on the second rope watched breathlessly as the three started down. We knew how close to exhaustion everyone was, and we worried over whether Houston would be able to climb. As we watched, he started off all right, but after going 20 feet he sat down in the middle of a steep snow patch, put his chin in his hand, and looked around as if to say, "What are we doing here?" Schoening looked perplexed. After a few moments he shook the rope and called down, "Come on, Charlie. Let's go!" And Charlie, still looking bewildered, got up and continued to climb down.

Perhaps this was a good time to have no inhibitions, for we were faced with a problem similar to climbing down a windswept, steeply slanted house roof, 1,700 feet long, with snow and ice covering many of the slates. The exposure was so severe that any slip would be hard to check and might pull the whole rope of men down off the mountain. We knew that we were physically exhausted and climbing under conditions that would have been extremely dangerous even when we were at our strongest. Each one of us had to climb with all the strength and skill he possessed. No one could slip.

The first rope had descended 100 yards and all were making good progress when the rest of us turned our backs on Camp VII and started to descend the relentlessly steep slopes. The storm clouds had risen a little, but the wind was sweeping great plumes of snow whirling across the rock slabs. Footing was dreadfully uncertain, and since Streather seemed strong, we had him go first. Next went Bell, whose uncertain steps because of his missing glasses and his frostbitten hands and feet were alarming, and finally came Molenaar and I. Molenaar's leg was bothering him but he kept as sound a belay as he could on Bell, and obviously did everything he could to secure me when I moved down behind him. We had moved down only a couple of rope lengths when we saw 100 feet to our right an ice ax sticking into a snow slope at a crazy angle. Molenaar made a careful traverse across the snow to reach it. It was Houston's ax, which had disappeared in the fall, and we quickly handed it over to Bell, whose ax had also vanished in his headlong plunge down the slope. This chance find helped Bell tremendously, for now with the ax he could probe places where he could not see clearly; but to watch George lean out over the slope and tap around with the tip of the ax was anything but reassuring to the other three men on the rope, who, standing on slabs covered with powder snow, were trying to safeguard the party. Under these conditions Bell's poise and steady climbing, despite his handicaps, were magnificent. He knew that his own life and ours were at stake, for we were all so near exhaustion that a slip could easily drag all four of us thousands of feet in a fall. And if Bell reached the point where he could not walk, we might be too weak to get him down.

In the back of our minds was the terrible lesson of the fatal storm on Nanga Parbat. We had more food on K2 than the Germans had had, but that wouldn't help if we couldn't reach it. Our feet and hands were numb as we cleared away the snow to find handholds and footholds. In some places the savage wind even helped us, for it had so firmed the snow that we could kick steps down it, but as a rule the powdery coating over the slabs did not adhere well, and climbing on this uncertain surface with such exposure below strained the firmest nerves. The accident of the day before and our miraculous rescue appeared to have developed in most of us a fatalistic attitude about our dangerous position. We had the feeling that matters were beyond our control. We seemed to be puppets pulled by a string, as if things were fated to happen in a certain way, do what we would, and nothing in the world could change them. Under the circumstances this fatalism, caused no doubt by the series of accidents of the past few days, was almost comforting, for we did not lose strength through nervous worry. We were doing our best. If that wasn't good enough, there was nothing else we could do to change things. What would be would be.

I have never had this fatalistic feeling before, but I certainly had it as we moved out onto the exposed col (pass) at the top of the steepest slope. Here, in an utter maelstrom of wind and whirling snow, we had to take off our crampons to climb down the smooth, steeply angled rock. We were already cold and as we eyed the slabs, which were here too steep for snow to cling, we faced a wind that was eddying furiously up the mountain directly at us. I have seldom been so cold.

With numb fingers we got George Bell's crampons off, pulled off our own, and then Streather climbed over the edge and disappeared. Thank God our fixed ropes there were clear of snow! But despite their help, this steep section of the descent seemed to take hours, and my feet had lost all sensation before the third man on the rope, Molenaar, reached a good belay point and called to me to start down from the col. Like the others, I could not move fast, but the blessed handlines helped, and putting my faith in the pitons that supported them, I stiffly lowered myself off that storm-swept col and onto the steep face. I still had confidence that we would get down that cliff, and on down to Camp VI. I wasn't going to worry, but I was terribly anxious to get all of us under shelter so we could start work to save our feet.

One at a time we moved down across the steep slabs, along the ridge and down another fixed rope on the other side. Here, on loose rocks precariously poised, we had a brief respite from the wind. Our strength was ebbing fast, and Molenaar, who had belayed so well above, was now climbing entirely on reserve strength and hardly able to take care of himself. At 200 feet from camp, Streather, the strongest man on our rope, climbed 20 feet down the wrong place and had to climb back. Reascending cost him frightful effort! Ahead was one more slippery traverse, but no one slipped, and after descending a shallow gully we stepped down almost onto the tents of Camp VI.

The others were already there when we arrived. They had found both tents full of snow, one of them right up to the top, for a couple of small rocks had fallen and made slits in one, and faulty closure of a zipper had provided a tiny opening in the other. Through these small entrances the driving monsoon winds had forced powder snow until the tents were drifted full.

Fortunately for us on the second rope, the others had just

finished clearing out the powder snow when we arrived, and they had started a stove. As we climbed into these tents, the most blessed sense of relief came over us. We had come down safely. We had passed the worst part of the route. Here were shelter and food. No matter how exhausted we were now, we had faith that we could get down.

Uncomfortable though we were, the next hours in camp seemed by contrast to be almost luxury. Charlie Houston seemed far more himself. Schoening and Craig reported that he had climbed extraordinarily well for a man in his condition, only occasionally sitting down in the most unexpected places and looking around as if to wonder what he was doing there. All of us looked years older than when we had been here before, but there was a confidence in our voices that had not been there that morning. Nobody made optimistic statements, but morale had improved.

While snow was melting for tea, we blew up the air mattresses which had not been abandoned above, arranged some 1939 sleeping bags we had found there, and took off our boots to work on our feet. My toes had no sensation, but neither did anybody else's, and I was glad to remember that my feet had not hindered my climbing down. Since the tent Houston and I were sharing stood in the lee of the other, and our tent had no holes that let in the wind, we called to George Bell to trade places with Bob Craig and move into the warmer tent. Bell's feet were a great worry to us now, for they were in the most dangerous condition of all. George shouted, "Okay," and started to crawl across the space between the tents. As he did so, he saw a little bag about 15 inches long and 8 inches high in the passage between the tents.

"Where did that come from?" he called, and without waiting for an answer he picked it up and pushed it into our tent ahead of him.

"Why, Tony found it about 1,000 feet below Camp VII," I said. "He thinks it's something of Art's. I haven't looked at it yet, but I'm going to take it to his family."

"It isn't Art's," said George huskily. "It's mine. It was in my pack when I lost it in the fall."

Eagerly he pulled at the zipper, drew it open, and began to fumble frantically inside. And now, to our utter amazement, George let out a gasp of joy and pulled forth his spare pair of eyeglasses—unbroken!

What the discovery did for Bell's morale we couldn't tell, but his delight did us all a lot of good. Also in the bag were the expedition accounts, for George was the field treasurer, but at that time we had no interest in such matters. The rest of his pack, however, with camera, exposed film, and diary, like Charlie Houston's, had completely disappeared, and we never saw it again.

All the way down, of course, we had been looking for Art Gilkey's body, but we never found it. We did see, however, a tangle of ropes and a broken ice ax about 1,000 feet below the ice gully where we had last seen him. The wooden shaft of the ax, broken in its fall down the mountain, had jammed between two rocks. Our friend must have had an instant and merciful death, the swift death that is the best kind, before his body was swallowed forever beneath the snows of the Karakoram.

That evening at six o'clock Charlie Houston was so far recovered that he could use the spare walkie-talkie, which was at Camp VI, to call Colonel Ata-Ullah at Base Camp. The emotion and relief in that good man's voice when he learned that we were alive was tremendous. "Thank God," he said, and for a moment or two he said little more. He had listened constantly since we had failed to keep our schedule with him at three o'clock the day before, and by now had practically given us up for dead. Next day he was planning to search the glaciers for us, and then, when weather permitted, climb as high as he could to look for us before accepting the fact that we were lost. He had told his fears to the Hunzas, and together they had had a mournful time.

That night at Camp VI we had a magnificent dinner of tomato soup, canned ham, rice, and cups and cups of tea, but darkness overtook us before the cups were cleaned and the sleeping bags arranged. Pushing aside the stove and dishes, Houston and I fell asleep almost before we could pull ourselves into the two parts of my sleeping bag, for Houston's bag, of course, had disappeared in the fall. Drugged as I was by exhaustion, my sleep was fitful, however, for Houston was out of his head again and all night long he kept getting out of the inner half of the sleeping bag, which he was using, and crawling about the tent. He was most anxious not to waken me and kept steadily apologizing for the trouble he was causing. "If I can just get out of this warehouse," he would say, "everything will be all right." Then, as best I could in the darkness, I would find the opening to his sleeping bag and try to get him inside. The next thing I knew, I would be awakened again by Houston crawling around the foot of my sleeping bag. "I'm terribly sorry to bother you," he would say. "If I can only get out of this warehouse. . . ."

Next morning the storm had increased in violence and we were apprehensive about starting down to Camp V for fear that George Bell would extend the damage already done to his feet. We were deeply worried about his condition. We feared that he might reach the point where he could not walk, and we hated to think what would happen then, for in our exhausted state and with a storm raging we could not carry anybody, let alone our biggest man, down along the ridges below. Since food and gasoline were short at Camp VI we were anxious to move some men down, and Schoening and Streather took advantage of a lull in the storm to push their way down to the next camp, but the lull ended and the rest of us stayed behind. Supplies of fuel were low and that night we went to bed with a cold supper and the realization that we had to start down again next day. Bell was now the main problem, for Houston was gaining strength and clarity of thought with remarkable rapidity.

August 13 was cold and windy with light snow falling, much like the day we had moved down to Camp VI. Craig and Molenaar had had a cold night in the torn tent, and after cold meat bars for breakfast, they pulled on their packs and started down. Putting George Bell in the torn tent for shelter, Houston and I began trying to free the bottom of the tent we were in from ice, for it was necessary for us to carry down one tent, and the other one was ripped. Our tent had become iced-in during previous use, and our hands became frightfully cold as we hacked at the ice and pulled at the knots. Meanwhile the wind was getting at the tent Craig and Molenaar had emptied, so that by the time we had freed the tent that was to go down, the wind had torn the other one from end to end with Bell in it, and the whole fabric began to shred apart as we huddled in it to try to bring back sensation to our nipped fingers. Then, swinging on heavy packs, we started down to Camp V.

To our delight, Bell climbed steadily and safely. The route from VI to V was normally not particularly difficult, but with fresh snow on the rocks some of the route was dangerously coated with loose snow, especially in one gully. Here Houston did a fine job of anchoring the rope as I went ahead. He seemed almost his old self as we moved down onto a tiny scree slope and around a corner into Camp V. Craig and Molenaar were already there, and they made way for us to move in where Schoening and Streather pumped the stove to a red-hot roar and poured cup after cup of orange juice–flavored tea down our still dehydrated throats. They had battled the storm the day before and had been glad to reach camp safely.

Our descent was going well now and the storm had let up a bit, but there was no indication that another frightful blow wasn't on the way. "If we can only get below House's Chimney," someone said, "it will take mighty bad weather to hold us back after that." We were still going on reserve energy and it was now about two-thirty in the afternoon, but the thought of putting the last major barrier behind us spurred us on. Normally we could climb from Camp V to the top of House's Chimney in five minutes, and from there look down on the tents of Camp IV almost directly beneath.

Now it took over an hour of the hardest work to get to the top of the chimney. Craig and Molenaar, who went ahead, shouted up to watch out for the ice, for everything was glazed over and there was great danger of a slip's pulling a whole rope of men off the mountain. We had heavier loads now, Houston especially, and we concentrated grimly on crossing this dangerously exposed section safely. Even so, Houston and I had a number of unpleasant moments and cut many steps before we climbed to the base of the A-frame and looked down the fixed rope Craig and Molenaar had set up in House's Chimney. And 150 feet below us we could see them working on the tents at Camp IV.

The hour was late enough so that not a moment could be wasted if we were to make the descent before dark. Houston insisted on belaying each man down in turn, and then we began to lower the packs to Schoening, who had climbed up the snow slope across from the foot of the chimney and made himself a platform there. These operations took time, for each pack had to be well secured, and it was almost dark when I climbed down the chimney and, guided by Schoening, crossed the ice steps to the rock outcrop from which we had hoisted loads three weeks earlier. Houston had been first man up the chimney and he wanted to be the last man down it, but it was nearly pitch-black by the time he left the tiny platform where he had been crouching so long and backed off the plunging cliff into space. Such a tangle of old and new ropes hung in the chimney that in the blackness the terrible thought swept over him that he was hanging on the wrong rope! Swinging out over this sheer cliff with the awesome gulf below is an impressive experience at any time, but it was doubly so to Houston, as with numb hands he launched himself out over the blackness, hoping that the rope was the right one and that it would reach the line of steps cut in the snow at the bottom.

The rope held, and Schoening was soon helping to guide Houston across the slope. A few minutes later we were all at the tent platforms of Camp IV, too tired to do more than swallow some tea, eat a cold meat bar for energy, and climb into our sleeping bags. Having House's Chimney behind us was a boost to our determination to get the whole party down safely. That night Molenaar, Houston, and I shared one tent, and I remember rubbing and rubbing to try to get feeling back into my toes. They didn't hurt and they weren't swollen, but try as I would, I couldn't bring back any sensation to some of my toes Still, the chimney, which had been long in our thoughts, was now behind us and we lay down scarcely conscious of the dampness of the half sleeping bag each of us was using.

When another gray dawn broke on August 14, gaunt, hollow-eyed men began to stumble out onto the slippery scree to collect pieces of ice to melt. Craig's feet were very painful but George Bell was an even greater worry, for he was obviously now going on nerve alone. This morning his feet were so swollen that he couldn't get his boots on no matter how hard he struggled, and at last he was forced to slit the boots with a knife in order to pull them on. These openings wouldn't increase his protection against further cold damage, but at least they would permit him to climb down with something on his feet.

This time Streather and I started down ahead to find and improve the route if possible. We found powder snow masking loose rocks and making part of our upward route unusable. Worse still, most of our fixed ropes were completely buried and we had to hack and hack to cut steps in smooth ice that covered slopes we had descended with ease before. Cutting steps straight down is arduous work, and both Streather and I were feeling the strain of the past few days. A couple of hundred yards above Camp III, we checked a slip before it got started, and then Schoening took over the lead to give us a rest and began cutting the last of the steps needed to get to camp.

How rich the air seemed! We had descended the equivalent of five Eiffel Towers, or ten Washington Monuments, below Camp VIII, and that part of the mountain already seemed impossibly remote. New York and home by contrast now seemed almost around the corner. But we were not down by any means. Storm clouds shrouded the slopes above us, and we knew that if the ice we had met just above Camp III plastered the route to Camp II, the next part of the descent would be especially dangerous, for the continuous strain was having its effect on all of us.

Camp III was well stocked with food, and since the wind had dropped, we made a solid lunch there. Like starving men, we gulped down date bars with almonds in them, chunks of Gruyère cheese, dried apricots, biscuits, and chocolate. We mixed a can of concentrated orange juice with snow, beat the icy mixture with a spoon until it grew mushy, and then took turns gulping great spoonfuls. Our bodies sorely needed replenishing with hot food and sleep, but Camp II was calling to us, for we knew that our faithful Hunzas would be there. Also, it was imperative that Bell waste no time in getting as low as possible, for we realized that before long, no matter how much nerve he had, he would be unable to walk on his frozen feet.

Ice over the rocks would make the route below Camp III very dangerous, and while we were pondering whether to descend or wait until the next day, Schoening moved down to the traverse across the first gully and found not ice but firm snow. We were much impressed, for we had expected more of the ice we had found just above. Morale soared. We even added to our packs a few items that had been left in duffel bags at Camp III, and then continued the descent.

This time Houston, Bell, and Schoening went first on one rope; Streather and I followed; and Craig and Molenaar brought up the rear. More than ever we were determined not to slip, and despite the need for one delicate maneuver after another, no one fell. Luckily the ice was not so bad as we had feared, and we gained confidence as we climbed down. The mountain took one parting shot at us, however, for just before Schoening, Bell, and Houston turned off the main slope into the shelter of a safe gully, a rock plummeting with great speed and noise from high on the mountain whizzed within a few feet of their heads.

Streather had the walkie-talkie, and exactly at six o'clock he tried to call Ata-Ullah. There was no flat place near us. Actually at exactly six I was standing on one foot traversing a steep rock wall, and didn't dare to move for fear of dislodging Streather, who was in an only slightly more secure position with one hand on the walkie-talkie. We hoped to tell Ata-Ullah to send porters next day to the glacier near Camp I to help Bell down, but Ata couldn't hear us and Streather finally folded in the radio aerial and went on.

As we started down the last couloir (gully) toward Camp II, we could hear the Hunzas shouting, and as we stepped onto the last snow slope, Ghulam, Vilyati, and Hidayat, roped together with what looked like string, swarmed out onto the steep slope and embraced us with tears rolling down their cheeks. It was an overwhelming welcome and almost too much for us in more ways than one, for we were clinging to small holds and standing at the top of a steep couloir which fell away 1,500 feet to the glacier below. Such a position is not suited to an uninhibited heart-to-heart embrace!

Our packs were taken from us and these hardy frontiersmen, with tears streaking their cheeks, handed us down from rock to rock as if afraid that at the last moment we would collapse. As each one of us reached Camp II, where sleeping bags had been laid out on the rocks for us to sit on, each Hunza in turn with great emotion embraced each one of us. The storm had ebbed away, the wind had dropped, and the first stars we had seen for weeks were glittering in the night sky as Craig and Molenaar climbed down the last rock pitch above camp.

Our feeling of relief and luxury at that moment is too great to describe. The ship had been saved; the lost, found. Every man who had started down from the dreadful bivouac at Camp VII had reached the safety of Camp II and the protection of our Hunzas. That evening was one of the sweetest any of us will ever spend, for a sense of supreme peacefulness enveloped us. Yet we were sad, too. We talked about Art Gilkey, and the Hunzas cried and prayed in unison for him. They wanted to know what had happened and how we had forced our way down through the storm.

And slowly as we lay there on sleeping bags with our boots

off in the warm, rich air, with a stove roaring cheerily *in the open* at our feet, we began to return to life. First the Hunzas fed us rice cooked in milk; then, with three stoves burning, we started on tea. Fuel and fire were plentiful here, and we made the most of it. Stacks of the flat pancakes called *chupattis* were cooked and pot after pot of tea and milk was brought over to us as we lay talking, relaxing, rubbing our feet, too emotionally stirred to go to bed. And all this while, kindly Hunza hands were kneading our tired muscles as only Asiatics can, bringing us back to life. At that heartwarming moment differences of race and language meant nothing. We and the Hunzas by the light of a flickering flare shared a great emotional experience as we talked and talked. Those who also have faced hardship and danger can appreciate our emotions and the bond between us all as we lay there. Then, after hours of delicious rest, we hoisted ourselves to our feet, staggered to our tents, and crawled gratefully into our sleeping bags. We had done it.

12 *Base Camp Again*

ROBERT H. BATES

When I woke from a sound sleep the next morning in a dry, whole sleeping bag, I heard a movement outside the tent door, and a minute or two later a Hunza handed in a cup of sweet tea. This simple act was a convincing demonstration that we were no longer fighting for our lives but were back on the fringes of civilization. And further proof was to come, for next a large batch of mail was thrust into the tent. The contrast was almost too much for us as we lay drinking tea, eating hot *pirattas* and reading letters, often many weeks old, full of love and well-wishes from our friends and families.

A hot sun, the first in weeks, was beating down, and its rays gradually drove us from the tents to sit in the warm, windless sunlight, mail in hand and the giants of the Karakoram, buried in new snow, looking down on us. Our cups literally and figuratively were very full. Except for the dull ache of Art Gilkey's loss, we felt at peace with the world. Our defeat did not rankle. We felt as if we had suffered and passed a very special test, an ordeal—why we did not know—but we had done our best and had survived.

While we sat on warm rocks, barehanded—even barefoot— reading mail and soaking in the sunlight, we realized that we were not quite down yet and we were still alarmed about the condition of George's frostbitten feet. Accordingly, after an appetizing breakfast in which the Hunzas joined, Streather and I were elected to go on ahead to Base Camp and send men up to the icefall with a stretcher to carry Bell back to camp. His feet looked frightful now, blistered and mottled in all shades of red and black. But George Bell is a stoic, and though he looked pale and on the verge of collapse, we knew that his iron will would keep him from complaining and drive him on down the mountain.

Streather and I found vast changes in the route as we worked our way down to the Godwin-Austen Glacier. In some places we found ice and were forced to chip out steps as we descended. Instead of going to Camp I, we tried a route the Hunzas had been using and headed down a long, steep scree slope to the edge of the glacier, then wound through a mass of séracs and crevasses until we came out on the relatively smooth ice of the center of the icefall. Here we were on our old route from Base Camp to Camp I and we made good time. Our toes felt strangely numb, however, and we walked stiffly.

We were trying to go fast, but neither of us could step out in a real stride, and rotten ice and uncertain stones made us put our feet down tenderly and a bit uncertainly. Not until we had skirted the snow fields below two hanging glaciers on the south face were we convinced that no traces of the fall from Camp VII would be found. And now our eyes turned toward the junction of the Godwin-Austen and Savoia Glaciers, for we could make out the tents of Base Camp a half mile ahead.

We could see figures about the tents, and soon some of the men came out to greet us. Our meeting was another heartwarming experience, for the simple coolies, whom we had joked with and encouraged on the march in to Base Camp, now threw their arms around us and with tears in their eyes told us how happy they were to see us return. One old rascal who had been with Shipton in the Sarpo Lago area during the Shaksgam Expedition was especially demonstrative and offered each of us a ride on his back. With this escort to accompany us, we walked on down the glacier, meeting Haji, the kindly leader of the porters, and other small groups of Baltis who had come up. Near camp,

Colonel Ata-Ullah came out to welcome us. We shook hands and embraced with a feeling of the closest fellowship, for here embodied was the voice we had heard so many times in our desperate position while snowbound on the mountain ledges high above. Here was our companion who had been at the other end of the walkie-talkie—in another world—sending us hope and encouragement and news, and providing a precious link with civilization and life itself.

Ata-Ullah had done some fine exploratory work while we had been gone and we viewed each other warmly and with increased respect. The camp itself illustrated Ata's efficient management, and in no time Streather and I were drinking tea, eating cheese and crackers, and telling of our experiences. "Thank God," Ata kept saying. "Thank God."

While we were talking, a stretcher party was organizing to go to the aid of our companions. George Bell we knew would need help, and there might be others. The colonel, of course, was going to lead this group, and fifteen minutes after our arrival the whole "rescue party" was clambering across the rock-strewn ice of the Godwin-Austen at top speed.

Their action was the signal for Streather and me to relax gratefully, and to look over more stacks of mail which had recently come in. Beria, labor disturbances in France—all seemed incredibly far away, interests of another world, and for the moment at least news that would normally strike our attention held no fascination. It was as if we had to learn our old set of values all over again.

Relaxing at Base Camp gave surprising pleasure to both of us, and although we made a few preparations for the arrival of the others, the release of pressure was so overpowering that we did little but drink tea, read mail, and let the Satpura men knead our leg muscles. At that moment we craved no delicacies, no entertainment, no luxuries. We felt like swimmers from a capsized boat who had just completed the long swim to shore. Merely being there was unspeakable luxury.

Late in the afternoon the others began to arrive. Schoening

was in the best shape of any, but he looked gaunt and haggard. Molenaar was limping and Houston's face showed the strain. Bob Craig was helped in by a Satpura man on one side and a Hunza on the other, while George Bell was borne in on a folding cot borrowed in June from Colonel Young in Rawalpindi for just such an emergency.

That night over pot after pot of tea we told and retold the events we had been too tired to discuss before. We were beginning to replace some of the liquid we had lost and all of us— Houston especially—had an almost unquenchable thirst. We were hungry, too, for though we had lost 10 to 20 pounds apiece, we had gained the greatest appetite of our lives. George Bell, who looked especially gaunt and emaciated, was particularly hungry, and though three of his toes were black, his good humor never failed. Like the rest of us, he appreciated the thoughtfulness of various Satpura porters, who kept bringing us such things as a few withered apples and a handful of dried apricots, carried all the way from Skardu. That they were deeply sympathetic was obvious.

The following morning we worked lethargically at packing our gear for the return trip. Nearly a third of the porters would be needed to carry George Bell, and we could not overload the others. Charlie Houston, who had blurred vision in his right eye from the blow on the head he had received on the mountain, worked hard on official mail despite his injuries. But the first letter he wrote was the most important. It was to Art Gilkey's father and mother in Ames, Iowa.

Art was very much in our thoughts as we boxed his personal belongings to send home, and about noon we gathered to pay him our respects for the last time. Under Colonel Ata-Ullah's direction the Hunza men had built a splendid cairn on a prominent point of rock at the juncture of the Savoia and Godwin-Austen Glaciers. It is a distinctive location, conspicuous to anyone approaching K2 from the south. From the cairn one can look down the Godwin-Austen to the vast ice amphitheater of Concordia and far beyond to the peaks of Ladakh. Less distant, the beautifully fluted snow slopes of Bride Peak rise gracefully, while across the valley gigantic Broad Peak towers. Past either side of the rock platform on which the cairn stands, the great glaciers coming down from the edge of China flow majestically. Beyond these icy highways to Savoia Pass and Windy Gap, the world of snow and rock seems endless, but most striking of all, behind the cairn, K2, awe-inspiring and immense, thrusts up toward the sky in a sweep of tremendous exaltation. It is well named the "mountaineer's mountain."

On wooden, tender feet we limped to the base of this 10-foot cairn and placed on it the aluminum box that had held Art Gilkey's personal effects. In it we reverently laid mountain flowers, a statement about our dear companion, the flags we had hoped to take to the summit, and a favorite poem. On top we placed his ice ax. Sadly, with bowed heads and heavy hearts, we read a passage from the Bible, said a prayer for our friend, and then with spirits somehow lifted, stumbled back toward camp. We stopped at the first tent to look around at the cairn, long to keep lonely vigil on the rock platform, and we realized again the uncertainty of all human endeavor and the relative permanence of the mountain giant on which the cairn stands.

AMERICAN ALPINE CLUB

THIRD KARAKORAM EXPEDITION
K2   1953

Dr. Charles S. Houston
Robert H. Bates
Exeter, N. H.

BASE CAMP   AUGUST 16 1953

This cairn is placed here in memory of Arthur K Gilkey
who was killed during a fall on K2 on August 10, 1953.

He was a gallant member of this expedition and a leader
in our attempt on the mountain.   His illness at 25,000
feet was an unexpected tragedy and his death during
our desperate attempt to rescue him is a loss which all
of us feel more keenly because of the closeness of
our bonds during the trying times.

[signatures]

13 *Out from the Mountain*

GEORGE I. BELL

On August 17 we began our trek away from the mountain. The clouds hung low over Base Camp as we prepared to leave at dawn, and we had no final view of K2. No doubt far above the Godwin-Austen Glacier and Base Camp, and above the lower camps of the Abruzzi Ridge, the savage, relentless winds still swept the heights of K2, derisively flapping the shreds of our tents. But far below these icy ledges, we on the glacier, the wreckage of an expedition, began the long trip home.

The eagerness and excitement with which we had approached Base Camp were gone. Bundled up in a sleeping bag, I was carried on a litter by relays of the strongest Satpuras. Houston trudged down the glacier in a set and trancelike manner, for the injury to his chest made normal movements of his arms and shoulders painful. Craig stumbled and tripped as he forced his tender feet to carry him along. Even Molenaar and Bates carefully favored their sore feet, while Streather and Schoening had no longer the brisk, free-swinging stride which is usually the mountaineer's joy.

On the mountain we had grown accustomed to looking forward to the trip out as something easy and rapid, and now as we left Base Camp, our motto was "Urdukas today." We all longed to see there the green grass and scrubby bushes of the last oasis. On our march in, the bandobast had taken three full days from Urdukas to Base Camp, but of course that had been days from Urdukas to Base Camp, but of course that had been uphill with 150 heterogeneous, unenthusiastic porters dragging their feet. Houston and Bates had told us how in 1938 the Base Camp cook, the well-beloved Ahdoo, had walked to Urdukas for wood and returned with his burden all in the same day. This feat suggested that with our band of stalwart Satpuras, we should easily reach Urdukas in a day. But the first evening found very tired sahibs and their porters less than half the distance to Urdukas. Indeed, during all the homeward march we made about the same distance per day as on the way in.

Of course, carrying me on the litter was extremely arduous for the Satpuras. Less than twenty of them were strong enough to be useful bearers, and even they could make only slow progress over the loose rocks and slippery glacial ice. But the walking wounded did not want to travel much faster than the litter bearers.

Each day between eight and twelve Satpuras would be chosen by their sirdar, Haji, or by some common consent to act as "dandy wallahs," for to them my litter was called a *dandy*. The number chosen depended on how hard they thought the day's travel would be. On the glacier, Hunzas, particularly Vilyati, Hidayat, and Ghulam, were usually at hand to chop steps and help the dandy wallahs in difficult spots. Ordinarily four men would carry the dandy for about fifteen minutes before being relieved by a second team.

My dandy was a lightweight canvas and steel cot, with each side reinforced by heavy bamboo poles, which had been brought for a large tent which the Hunzas used. The poles were lashed to the sides of the cot with Balti goat-hair ropes, and extended far enough past each end of the cot so that four men could carry the dandy on their shoulders. I lay on the litter either in or on a sleeping bag, and was tied on with a few turns of goat-hair rope. The steel framework of the cot was flexible and gave the dandy an easy-riding, knee-action quality.

The Baltoro Glacier and Braldu Valley, however, were not laid out with an eye to comfortable travel. The glacier above

Urdukas offered comparatively good going and only in a few places did the dandy wallahs have great difficulties. But from Urdukas on, the track became frequently too narrow, steep, or tortuous for four men or virtually any number to maneuver the litter. In these situations, the courage and strength of a small group of Satpuras proved my salvation. Indeed, from Urdukas on I spent about one-third of the time being carried piggyback by one stout Satpura or another.

The need first arose shortly beyond Urdukas, where the track entered a V-shaped trench between the moraine and a rock wall. The trench did not give the dandy wallahs room to maneuver, and soon a few obstructing boulders brought progress to a complete halt. At this point the biggest and strongest of the Satpuras took off his shoes, knelt down beside the litter, and with a gentle smile invited me to climb aboard. His name was Mohammed Hussein, but we did not know this for a while and called him John Ridd, after the strong-man hero of *Lorna Doone.* When I had secured a good hold on his broad shoulders, John rose to his feet without visible effort and began with wonderful balance to traverse the tortuous route. Sprawled on his back with my arms draped over his shoulders and clasped across his chest, I could peer over his shoulder and see exactly what went on. John for his part seldom used his hands for balance and usually held my knees with a firm grip. And so in this position he strode from boulder to boulder, balanced across narrow, muddy ledges or, wonder enough for me, walked unflinchingly across a stretch of sharp stones. Each time he carried me, John would remove his shoes so as to obtain better purchase on the often minute and insecure footholds, and in time I came to feel almost as secure on his strong back as I had on my own two feet during the march in.

Big John was a young and gentle strong man. Each time he put me down after a hard carry, he would turn around with a sympathetic boyish grin and inquire, *"Tik, sahib?"* (Everything okay, sahib?) It was impossible not to say yes. For all his strength, John liked nothing better than to sing in a high falsetto voice and go through a bit of a dance for his comrades.

Zafar Ali was perhaps not the second strongest Satpura, but he wouldn't admit this for all the world. He spoke a great deal and acted out each sentence with his fine mobile features and expressive gestures. He was an enthusiastic man and zealously took on his role as second strongest sahib carrier. Certainly Zafar Ali was the most comfortable riding Satpura, for in his pride he held me high up on his shoulders so that I barely needed to hold on. Zafar Ali had something of the Arabian Nights about him, something like Shah Khan, the Hunza leader we had met in Skardu. These were glamorous men. My estimate of them was colored by imagination, but it was easy to visualize them leading a band of trusted followers over the edge of the world.

The other Satpuras were less certain of their abilities and undertook to carry my shrunken frame, now about 170 pounds, with less assurance. Smallest, most cheerful and courageous of the select band was Taki, whom we christened Smiley. For some reason, Smiley was clothed more or less in city-made rags, while most of the Satpuras wore homespun. Perhaps he had traveled more to acquire his Bohemian air. The two other strongest carriers came into their own only after Big John, Zafar Ali, and Smiley had carried me on several successive days and proved that the labor could be borne.

My own feelings about being carried by litter and piggyback were mingled. Most pronounced was resignation: this was, after all, the only way to get out of the mountains. But I counted the days, eleven in all. My arms would go to sleep clutched over the shoulders of the carrier, his back and shoulders would grow weary and sore, but each ten-minute carry, which was about what Big John did in his prime, or each two- or three-minute stretch, which was about par for the others, brought us that much closer to the goatskin raft, the zahk which would float us down the Shigar River to Skardu.

I always had the feeling that except for temporarily useless feet, I was essentially a healthy man. True, my fingers were lacking skin and swollen, but they were improving every day. I was also weak, but I had a good appetite, which has often seemed to me a good criterion of health. My feet did not hurt enough to bother me so long as anything interesting was happening, but at night Bob Craig and I often would be kept awake by our feet.

Each morning Houston would hold sick call. He could do little for himself, but he would always wash my toes in soap and hot water, rebandage them, and give me a shot of penicillin. A couple of times really sick people showed up to destroy any illusion of real physical misfortune that I might have. The second day out of Base Camp, one of the most cheerful of the Satpuras approached Charlie with a wry turn to his accustomed grin, complaining of headache and cough. He was given an aspirin or something similar. By the time we reached Urdukas the next day, however, he was very much worse, racked by a deep cough, and barely conscious of his surroundings. Charlie diagnosed pneumonia, shot him full of penicillin, and probably saved his life. Two days later, to our utter amazement, the near casualty wore his cheerful grin again and insisted on carrying a full load.

The attitudes of our porters toward Charlie's needle were strong and varied. One old reprobate with an infected gum was greatly disappointed when he recovered and could no longer be stuck with the potent needle. But later a younger Satpura with an infected finger fled in terror when Charlie approached with the needle, and no amount of persuasion could induce him to submit to treatment.

Most of the patients at sick call had vague complaints and were apparently looking for free pills. Others from villages we passed through came with little hope. For instance, once a father appeared before Charlie carrying his lovely young daughter of about thirteen in his arms. Some weeks before she had been playing in a high tree, had fallen, and since then had been unable to walk or move her legs at all.

On the route from Urdukas to Askole, we had much difficult

travel. At first the chaotic, boulder-strewn glacier at times must have caused my carriers to wonder what they had done to be cursed even in this life with such burdens. Perhaps this is not orthodox Moslem reasoning, but I should think the sentiment inevitable. When we had escaped from the barren chaos which men call the Baltoro Glacier, the dandy wallahs and I grinned at each other with mutual pleasure.

Beyond the glacier our way lay close beside the raging Braldu River. Often we saw no suggestion of a trail; but only a precarious system of ledges, which even an unladen man might eye with misgivings. Here Mohammed Hussein was invaluable and I often wondered what would happen to me without him. In time, when Mohammed was sick for a few days, I learned that other Satpuras, inferior in strength perhaps but not in courage, would carry me on.

The first rope bridge posed an interesting problem. Needless to say, no one was particularly eager to carry me across, nor was I particularly eager to be carried across. The Satpuras crossed the bridge to eat a meal on the other side, perhaps thinking that if the problem was ignored for a bit it would vanish. Mohammed Hussein was frankly terrified by rope bridges. Zafar Ali had waved good-by to me with a wry smile and copious gestures to the effect, "Just wait a little while, sahib, and I will be back to carry you over with no trouble at all." But before he returned, Houston and Craig came over with a pair of thick felt overshoes which belonged to Ata and I tried to cross the bridge on my own. The struggle turned out to be much easier than we had expected. The side ropes or railings were low, so that I could sit on the center strands and still hold on to the side ropes firmly. I then progressed by placing my weight on my arms and heels in front and shifting forward to sit a little farther along on the bridge. Bob Craig went ahead to spread the side ropes appropriately, and in this manner I crossed the first rope bridge without even breaking my blisters.

The two subsequent bridges below Askole were not so easy because their side ropes were higher and could not be reached while sitting down. Hence a certain amount of more or less upright walking was necessary, and the rushing torrent beneath proved a more than adequate stimulus. Truthfully, I cannot think back on the crossing of the rope bridges as entirely unpleasant. After all, in these places I was able to do something for myself above and beyond merely emulating a sack of potatoes.

Beyond the last rope bridge, two extremely grueling days were needed to traverse the rock walls of the desolate Braldu Valley. At times the trail lay along banks of crumbling rubble close beside the foaming water; then it would climb a disintegrating wall of glacial debris to circumvent a precipice. The first day was backbreaking labor, and the dandy wallahs swore they could do no more. Accordingly, for the last day we enlisted the help of six strong men from a nearby village, who together with Zafar Ali, Taki, Rustum, Hassan, and Mohammed Hussein succeeded in hauling me over a last fearful section to Niyil, close to the goatskin zahk.

We had all been sure that the trip out would be much faster and easier than the journey in. Some of us had even toyed with the idea of making interesting side trips, such as a short detour to look at a ridge on the fabled Mustagh Tower, a ridge which the eye of faith might construe to be a possible route. Craig wanted to spend some days in Hunza getting better acquainted with that friendly land, its people, and its Hunza *pani*—literally Hunza "water," but actually wine. Art Gilkey and I had planned to relax on a houseboat in the Vale of Kashmir.

The reality was, of course, a far cry from these dreams, but we had certain compensations. The terrible days of storm, struggle, and death high on K2 had welded us together with a bond which was hard at the time to appreciate. There had been other pressing preoccupations then, and it was only when we had escaped the inhuman world of the wind and heights that we could appreciate in some leisure the depths of common experience and understanding which were ours. When men climb on a great mountain together, the rope between them is more than a mere physical aid to the ascent; it is a symbol of the spirit of tbe enterprise. It is a symbol of men banded together in a common effort of will and strength—not against this or that imagined foeman of the instant, but against their only true enemies: inertia, cowardice, greed, ignorance, and all weaknesses of the spirit. These things were hard to realize at the time. It was only in some tranquillity and leisure that we who together had ventured far and nearly lost all could appreciate what had happened.

Each time we got together for breakfast or dinner on the homeward trip was a memorable occasion. At first, as at Camp II and at Base Camp, merely being able to sit down and eat enough and drink enough and be together seemed heavenly. This was a stage when all we seemed to be able to do was to recount over and over again what had happened above, letting no detail escape us. And when the wholly remarkable facts had settled to the bottom and no longer needed to be retold at each gathering, there remained the warmth of comradeship. It is sad that usually such a spirit arises among men only in war. Charlie Houston put it well when he said, "We entered the mountains as strangers, but we left as brothers."

Forgotten delicacies appeared to make the meals memorable as we came to Askole and other villages. We stuffed ourselves with apricots, chickens, eggs, grapes, apples, pears, and cucumbers, for the fertile valley was yielding luxuries unknown to the grim regions beyond. I can remember lunch on the day when we were supposed to reach Askole. A few days previously some of the Askole men had been sent ahead to bring back atta for the Satpuras. They brought it and also some dainties for the sahibs. The going had been hard and the dandy wallahs and I were far in the rear of the bandobast when we came upon Ghulam and Haji Beg with "lunch for the sahib." My lunch turned out to be ten hard-boiled eggs, two small chickens, and chuppatis. The dandy wallahs were perhaps a bit depressed by seeing me eat with such gusto, but that did not detract from my enjoyment of the entire meal. At Chokpyong and Niyil, the apricots were just ripe and we made hogs of ourselves. I can recall Tony reclining against a tree, helping himself for the fiftieth time to a large basket of apricots with a wistful "I shall very likely be sick tomorrow, but. . . ." And then at Yuno, just before the zahk voyage, we had a king's feast of apricot seeds, dried mulberries, cucumbers, and grapes.

At Askole, Ata, Schoening, and Bob Bates diverged from the Braldu Gorge to take a short cut over a 16,400-foot pass, the Skoro-La, and thence go directly down to Shigar. This would save them three days' travel and offer splendid views of peaks along the Braldu. Their trip was favored by perfect weather which, if it was clear back in the high peaks, was the first pleasant weather there in well over a month. Ata was impatient, as his leave was coming to an end, and he spurred his party to a rapid crossing.

Meanwhile the rest of us marched and lived for the day when we would come to the zahk (goatskin raft) which we were certain wouhd carry us in painless splendor the remaining 50 or so miles to Skardu. We were supposed to meet the zahk at Niyil, where we had first crossed the Braldu on the way in. The river was high, however, and so we spent the better part of another day climbing up and down along the Braldu.

The Satpuras could almost see where their home village lay as we swung into the wide Shigar Valley. Their hearts were cheered, and every now and then they would break into song. Their favorite was a sort of leader and chorus ballad, where Mohammed Hussein would chant something in a high falsetto, and the others would join in on the refrain. I have no idea what these songs were about, but very likely the Satpuras recalled their women, children, homes, and fields, which they would soon see again after their long, hard journey into the great mountains.

The zahk wallahs soon appeared and ferried everyone over to Yuno on the other side of the Shigar. This crossing was no mean feat in itself, for here the river was divided into many turbulent channels, each one of which was a powerful stream. But the zahk wallahs were Yuno wallahs as well, and at home in these channels.

August 29 was the day of our great zahk ride. This particular zahk was made of about thirty goatskins and floated high and easy with its eight passengers: Houston, Streather, Molenaar, Bob Craig, and me, and the three zahk wallahs. Oldest and most experienced zahk wallah was a small, gray-haired Balti, who looked just the part of a river pilot. After a leisurely start, we soon found ourselves bobbing down to Shigar at about 10 knots. The multitudinous channels of the Shigar River sprawled over an extensive gravel plain, and the zahk wallahs skillfully poled and paddled their craft, striving to keep it where the water flowed swift but not heavy. A few times we ran some fair rapids and once we nearly grounded, but on the whole the travel was smooth. Lulled by the warm sun and easy motion, our spirits were high. Charlie spoke of 1938, and how in that year two expedition zahks had held the first Harvard-Yale zahk race on the Shigar, a race which (as I recall) Harvard was winning by several lengths until their zahk ran aground. Displaying my scientific background, I convinced Bob Craig that the cup of water which he was drinking from the Shigar River almost certainly contained atoms from the first glass of water that he had ever had in his life. And Tony told another of his great tales of life on the Northwest Frontier before partition.

Three times the zahk pulled in to shore for minor repairs, mostly the blowing up of goatskins which were becoming deflated. Below the village of Shigar, the river was confined in only one or two big channels, and here we made rapid progress. In the afternoon, the huge rock outcrops by Skardu came in sight. Soon we approached the confluence of the Shigar with the great Indus River. Their waters met in conflict and turmoil, but our old river pilot and crew treated the place with caution and safely brought the zahk to the far side of the Indus, whence Skardu was only about a mile away. Two farmers were enlisted to carry me to Skardu. Since darkness was coming on, Houston and Molenaar hurried ahead to get a regular litter and bearers from the hospital, but my two carriers proved so strong that I reached the hospital before the litter bearers were organized, and indeed quite a while before Bob Craig could hobble in.

Thus, after long travail, we were returned to the world of men. The new, young, and energetic political agent gave us a delicious curry, and soon I was comfortably ensconced in a bed of the civil and military hospital.

The next day we said good-by to the Hunzas, who had stood by us so faithfully during the entire course of the expedition. "Perhaps we shall come again," we said.

"Or I shall go to America," answered Hidayat with his most infectious smile.

On August 31 we boarded an Orient Airways DC-3 and flew to Rawalpindi, where Charlie's wife, Dorcas, had traveled half-way round the world to meet him. The Indus Canyon was as spectacular as before. When the pilot took the DC-3 up to 20,000 feet we could see close by such mighty summits as Rakaposhi, Haramosh, and the high and deadly Nanga Parbat, which had finally been climbed only two months before by a German-Austrian party.

Far, far in the distance there stretched out jagged range upon range of storybook mountains, and above all the others the symmetrical, ice-encrusted, and wind-swept summit pyramid of K2.

Afterword

For me K2 1938 remains a bittersweet memory of a great adventure. My physical injuries healed rapidly; the emotional wounds left deeper scars. I remember only vivid fragments of those ten days in August, but the rest of our odyssey is deeply etched in my mind.

When I lay unconscious after the fall, Bob had roused me by recalling my wife, Dorcas, and our children. Once home again, I slowly recognized that they were the center of my world. But life went on. For the next eight months Bob and I were furiously busy with film to edit, articles to write, and lectures to give to raise money to pay our debts. In December we began this book. We each had full-time jobs. It was not the time to think about another expedition.

However, the seed was there, and I sought and obtained permission for another attempt in 1955. In Rawalpindi, on our way home, we had met Ardito Desio, and in August, 1954, his large Italian expedition did reach the summit. This had two impacts on me: I was disappointed that "our" mountain had been climbed, and almost for the first time I came to see how close I had been to death, and what this would mean to my family. I declined my permit for 1955.

Soon, seeking a larger world, I persuaded Dorcas that I should accept an invitation to direct an idealistic medical program in Aspen, Colorado. A few years later, a mountain rescue catapulted me into a career in mountain medicine and physiology. Then Bob and Sargent Shriver persuaded me to be director of the Peace Corps in India, an unforgettable experience for my whole family. In 1966 I became a professor at the University of Vermont. Each summer from 1967 to 1979 I directed a high-altitude research program in the Yukon, and in 1985 I ran a repeat of the acclimatization study called Operation Everest, first done in 1946. I've published many medical papers and several books, and have been active in mountain medicine ever since—but not in climbing.

Over the years the ties which held our little band together in August 1953 have strengthened. Before the expedition, Bob and I had selected our companions for their character and personalities rather than for their climbing brilliance. They were all good climbers, of course, but even more—they were people we liked, people we felt intuitively we could rely on, men of character. We had not been mistaken. Those qualities had saved our lives.

The first weeks in August, 1953, inexorably changed my life. I lost interest in attempting the great mountains, perhaps because, as the prime mover for the expedition, and also the doctor, I felt I had failed. We had not reached the summit, and I had been unable to save our friend's life. That our peers have praised us for actions which we saw implicit in the mountain spirit was irrelevant. I turned to teaching and practicing medicine, and to research and writing about high altitude. For me, K2 1953, though a failure, was my personal epiphany.

Charles S. Houston
Burlington, Vermont
1994

I returned from K2 somewhat stunned, feeling that we had escaped a malevolent storm that had us by the throat and tried to kill us. Afterward, I told myself that nothing would ever scare me again, for I had survived something worse. I had not lost my love of mountains or interest in climbing, but I was ready for more important matters. In 1954 Gail Oberlin and I were married and, thanks to a sabbatical leave from Phillips Exeter Academy, began our marriage with a leisurely trip around the world, including Nepal, a country we were to know better.

Back in Exeter, I concentrated on being a teacher, with activities that included the ski team, the mountaineering club, the Exeter Social Service Organization, and committees of the town. The American Alpine Club, where Gail had been the secretary and I was a member of the board, however, was still a major interest, and in 1959 I began a three-year term as president (becoming the honorary president, a lifetime position, many years later).

In 1962 Sargent Shriver asked me to be the first Peace Corps director in Nepal, a country then little known to foreigners. Not long after our return, another leave permitted me to help Joshua Miner organize and develop Outward Bound in the United States.

Gail and I have traveled widely, frequently in mountain areas, and in 1974, with Ann and Adams Carter, returned to the K2 base camp. In 1985 Nicholas Clinch and I formed a joint Chinese-American expedition to travel to "the Great Ice Mountain" (the Ulugh Muztagh) on the Sinjiang-Tibet border, a peak that had been shown on world maps for 90 years as 25,340 feet high. Our team climbed it, but a satellite survey we carried out showed its true height to be just under 23,000 feet.

I have written four books, two with Charlie Houston, all in some way having to do with mountains. The last, *The Love of Mountains Is Best*, is being published in 1994.

Exciting moments are no stranger to me, but only once has my mind and body been so completely focused that I seemed to live 100 years in ten days. That was when our great quest for K2, so near success, became a life-and-death struggle for survival.

Robert H. Bates
Exeter, New Hampshire
1994

1 *Biographies*

Arthur K. Gilkey

[Largely excerpted from the April–May, 1961, issue of *The Iowan* magazine.]

After Art Gilkey died, his family received nearly 500 letters, many from eminent geologists who were shocked by the loss of one of the most promising scholars in the field.

Art achieved much in his 27 years. He grew up in Ames, Iowa, where his father headed the Department of Theoretical and Applied Mechanics at Iowa State College. After three years of high school he entered Iowa State but enlisted in the Navy after his freshman year and served 22 months as a radio technician. Vacations were spent in the Tetons or Sierras, and in 1947 after his return to college he made the sixth official ascent of Devil's Tower in Wyoming. The following summer Art held an assistantship in the Tetons, as he did again in 1949.

Following graduation, Art was offered assistantships at Harvard, Johns Hopkins, and Columbia. He chose Columbia, where he majored in structural geology. In 1950 he was with the Juneau Icefield Project in Alaska and the next summer in an Atomic Energy Commission program in New Mexico. In 1952 he led the American Geographical Society program in the

Juneau Icefield. At the time of his departure for K2 he had completed his thesis but had not put it in final form. Columbia University awarded the Ph.D. posthumously and also established a book collection in his memory.

Among many tributes to our lost friend are these: the Gilkey Fund, established by the American Alpine Club to help scientists who are working in mountain areas; the Gilkey Glacier, 16 miles long, named in recognition of his work in Alaska; Cerro Gilkey in the Chilean Andes, named for him by Polish and Argentine climbers, who wrote:

"When we read about the American attempt on K2, we were profoundly impressed by the magnificent spirit that prevailed in that expedition. But what impressed us more was the great comradeship: the fact that all climbers stood by Arthur Gilkey when his life was in danger is what inspired us most, for that spirit is one of the most sacred values of mountaineering. Therefore, although we weren't acquainted with Arthur, we felt we had to honor in some way such splendid comradeship. And that's how we came to naming one of the beautiful Patagonian summits with the name of Art Gilkey."

We will always miss him.

H.R.A. Streather

Tony Streather, a career army officer, has had notable military and mountaineering careers, often successfully blending the two. He has been on active duty in many "hot spots" around the world, including Korea, for which he was awarded the Order of the British Empire for action with the Gloucesters, a regiment he later commanded. In 1955 he made the first ascent of Kangchenjunga, the world's third highest mountain. Two years later he led an Oxford University expedition to Haramosh which ended in tragedy, described in *The Last Blue Mountain* by Ralph Barker. In 1976 he led a British Army expedition to Mount Everest, and several members of the party reached the summit. He has been active in Outward Bound and continues to help develop mountaineering skills and ethics among young people. He was president of the Alpine Club from 1992 to 1994. He retired as a lieutenant colonel, and he and his wife live in Wiltshire.

Robert W. Craig

Despite his frostbitten feet on K2, Bob Craig continues to ski and climb. In 1973 he and Schoening led a group of American climbers to participate in a Soviet climbing camp in the Pamirs. His book *Storm and Sorrow* describes his near death in an avalanche triggered by an earthquake, as well as the terrible storm which killed eight Soviet women. Next, he led a party attempting the Northeast Ridge of Mount Everest, only to be turned back by storm. He continues to climb in many parts of the United States and in 1983–1986 was president of the American Alpine Club.

Craig has long been involved in solutions for the contemporary problems of society, for eleven years with the Aspen Institute for Humanistic Studies and, since 1975, as founder and director of the Keystone Center, in Keystone, Colorado.

Mohammad Ata-Ullah

In 1954 Mohammad Ata-Ullah was liaison officer with the Italian party that climbed K2, and in 1960 his autobiography, *Citizen of Two Worlds*, described his remarkable life as Army officer, ophthalmologist, and mountaineer. He next studied engineering and became a partner in a Yugoslavian firm before developing his own construction company in 1967, which worked on major projects throughout Pakistan. He handed this over to his sons, retired, and learned to fly and to play the piano. In 1969 he headed a major study to reorganize Pakistan's health care system, for which he was decorated. He remained fit and active until 1972, when he died from carbon monoxide poisoning due to a defective space heater in his hotel room.

Peter Schoening

Pete Schoening was married shortly after our return and has several children and grandchildren. He has built a successful company, Chem-Grate Inc., of which he is now president, with offices in the United States, Germany, and China. Pete has an extraordinary record of climbs, including Hidden Peak in 1958, the first 8,000-meter peak climbed by an American, and Mount Vinson in 1968, the highest peak in Antarctica. In 1975 he and Bob Craig led an American group to join Soviet climbers in the Pamirs, and in 1985 he was with Bob Bates on a Chinese-American expedition which made the first ascent of Ulugh Mustagh (the Great Ice Mountain) on the northern border of Tibet. He suffered severe frostbite during a dramatic rescue on Mount McKinley, but continues to climb in the Rockies, Alaska, and China. He and his wife live in Bothell, Washington,

Dee Molenaar

Dee Molenaar remarried shortly after his return in 1953 and worked for the U.S. Geological Survey on water resources until his retirement. He then was able to give full time to his passion—painting mountain scenes and making beautiful maps. His skill places him among the leading mountain artists in the country. He does many climbs in the Rockies, and several editions of his book on Mount Rainier have been printed. He is currently finishing his autobiography, a narrative of forty years of mountaineering and art.

George I. Bell

George Bell lost only a portion of two toes from frostbite and soon returned to his position in theoretical physics at Los Alamos, where he lives today. He became active in theoretical biological systems, specializing in genetic engineering, and has led the genome project at Los Alamos for the last few years, publishing several important medical papers on genetic engineering. His injuries did not keep him from climbing. In 1955 he climbed high on Mount Lhotse and made several first ascents in the Lhotse-Kangtega area of Nepal. George was one of the summiters on Masherbrum, a peak we often admired from K2. He and his wife, Ginny, have trekked and climbed extensively in Nepal, Pakistan, Bhutan, China, South America, and Russia.

THE AUTHORS

Charles Houston

Charles Houston was born in New York City in 1913, graduating from Harvard College in 1935 and from Columbia University College of Medicine in 1939. After a two-year internship at Presbyterian Hospital, he married Dorcas Tiemeyer and was commissioned in the Navy during the summer of 1941. He received his flight surgeon's wings just prior to Pearl Harbor and for the next five years was engaged in high-altitude training and research. His final work in the Navy was a study named Operation Everest, which demonstrated that acclimatized men could survive and work as high as or even higher than the top of Mount Everest.

From 1947 to 1957 he practiced medicine in Exeter, New Hampshire, and from 1957 to 1962 in Aspen, Colorado. In 1962 he became director of the Peace Corps in India, until 1965. After a year in Washington, he accepted a professorship at the University of Vermont, where he now lives.

Houston was introduced to mountaineering in 1925, when his family took him to the Alps. Later he went to Alaska with Brad Washburn and in 1934, with his father, made the first ascent of Mount Foraker. In 1936 he helped organize a British American party which climbed Nanda Devi in India, and in 1938 he was back in India, attempting K2 with Bob Bates. In 1950 he and his father were the first westerners to examine the Nepalese side of Mount Everest, and in 1953 he returned to K2. In 1991 he visited Nanga Parbat with a British film crew.

Since 1941 he has been active in mountain medicine. From 1967 to 1979 he directed a summer research study on Mount Logan (Canadian Yukon), and in 1985 he directed Operation Everest II, an expanded version of the 1947 project. He has published five books and many articles about high altitude.

He and his wife, Dorcas, live in Burlington, Vermont. His three children are scattered about the country, and his son Robin is a doctor and a world-class mountaineer.

Robert H. Bates

Robert H. Bates, born in Philadelphia in 1911, started to climb as a boy during summers in Maine and New Hampshire. His serious climbing began in the Fairweather Range of Alaska in 1932–1933, with his Harvard classmate Bradford Washburn, and it led to a life of exploratory mountaineering whenever his academic career permitted. He was graduated from Harvard in 1933 and took an M.A. there in 1934. In the fall he was offered a job as instructor in English at the University of Pennsylvania, but when he arrived there was no job. Too many students had withdrawn because of the Depression. He began graduate work for a Ph.D., but when Washburn offered him a place on a winter National Geographic Society Expedition exploring and surveying in Yukon Territory's Saint Elias Mountains, he joyfully accepted it. He returned to begin teaching at the University in the fall of 1935.

He taught for four years at Pennsylvania, then left in 1939 to begin a less formal style of teaching at Phillips Exeter Academy in New Hampshire, his old school, where he would remain for 37 years. Meanwhile, he had not lost his interest in mountain climbs and exploration. In 1936 he did research at Oxford University, following it with climbs in the Alps, and the next year, with Washburn, he ascended what had been the highest unclimbed mountain in North America, Mount Lucania (17,150 feet) in the Saint Elias Mountains. He was then invited to join the First American Karakoram Expedition to K2, led by Charlie Houston. The expedition discovered the best route up the mountain and, though they failed to reach the top, climbed several thousand feet higher on K2 than anyone previously. (See *Five Miles High*, by members of the expedition, ed. Bates.)

In 1941 Bates and Walter Wood, who were planning an American Geographical Society Expedition to the Saint Elias Mountains, were asked to use the expedition to test clothing and equipment for the U.S. Army. On their return, Exeter released Bates to the War Department, where he became a consultant after Pearl Harbor and was commissioned as a captain and assigned to the Quartermaster General's Office. As executive officer of the Alaskan Test Expedition in 1942, he made the third ascent of Mount McKinley while testing clothing and equipment. In 1944, in combat at Anzio, he conducted an important test of newly developed items. He was in Italy, working on body armor, when the European part of World War II ended.

After his five years in the Army, Bates finished his work for the Ph.D. before returning to Exeter. (His thesis topic was *The Literature of the Mountains*). His last climbing in Alaska came in 1951, when he made first ascents of Mounts Alverstone and Hubbard, two big boundary peaks. In 1953 he went back to K2 with Charlie Houston, as described in this book.

Now retired, but not too old to travel, he lives happily in Exeter, New Hampshire.

2 *Then and Now*

NOW THAT ALL the great mountains have been climbed many times and by many different routes, exploratory mountaineering has practically disappeared. Thousands climb in all parts of the world, on extreme rock, steep and dangerous ice, and snow. Some climb alone, some climb "alpine style"—rushing the summit in a day or two—and fewer use the conservative "siege tactics" of the past. Aids like ice and rock pitons, karabiners and jumars, and miles of fixed rope are used to make the most difficult pitches safer and faster. Artificial climbing walls and speed climbing competitions are common, creating a new and different sport. Mountaineering as we knew it fifty years ago is quite different today.

However, comparisons between our pioneering 1938 attempt and modern expeditions have some poignant interest, if only for readers with nostalgia for "the good old days."

TRAVEL

In 1938 one went by sea from the U.S. to Europe and on to Asia, though there were occasional flights (with many stops) from Europe to India. We took almost four weeks to travel by boat to Bombay and by train to Kashmir. This was before partition of the subcontinent into India and Pakistan, and we walked 350 miles from Srinagar to Base Camp. It was in itself a great adventure, giving us excellent conditioning and a chance to know each other very well indeed. After the climb we took a shorter route back to Kashmir. The total cost of travel from home to Base Camp and back was $3,800 for eight persons.

By 1953 one could fly the Atlantic and on to India or Pakistan in a few days, though starting the march from Kashmir to the mountain was not possible due to the border conflict. Instead we flew from Rawalpindi in Pakistan to Skardu, leaving only 150 miles to walk to Base Camp. Afterwards we limped slowly back to Skardu, carrying our injured, and then flew to Rawalpindi and home. All our round-trip travel cost roughly $14,200. (This was actually a little less than our costs in 1938, for $1 in 1938 was the equivalent of $5.38 in 1953 and is the equivalent of $10.25 today.)

Today one can fly directly to Pakistan and to Skardu, and take jeeps to Askole, leaving only a week of walking. Evacuation of the injured can be arranged (at great cost) by helicopter. Those in a hurry can reach Base Camp from the U.S. in two weeks or less, missing much of the joy and excitement of the march to the mountain. Per person the round trip from home to mountain can total $40,000, as it does for one person on an expedition to Everest, and even more for one to K2.

TRANSPORT

Costs of moving the expedition baggage to Base Camp are difficult to compare because of the great differences in travel time. In 1938 almost everything was shipped from the U.S. to India and carried on horses or by porters from Kashmir to Base Camp. From there to Base Camp took more than three months. For the first few marches we used twenty-five ponies; from Skardu we had seventy to eighty porters. Six Sherpas came from Darjeeling. They climbed wonderfully well with us to the next-to-last camp. All this cost $1,500. The Sherpas' wages came to $400.

By contrast, in 1953 the cost of freight, porters, and their food came to $9,300 and transport took eight weeks from the U.S. to Base Camp. We hired 125 to 180 porters, depending on the march, and six Hunza men, since Sherpas, coming from India, could not be used in Pakistan. The Hunzas were tough and used to mountains, but they were untrained, and we dared not use them above Camp III.

All the above costs are in the dollars of those times.

In 1954 the Italian expedition of twenty climbers (two of whom reached the summit) cost over one hundred million lire, included more than two dozen expert climbers, and used 502 porters to take them to Base Camp.

Today many expeditions travel more lightly and fly with their equipment. Much food and equipment can be purchased in Nepal and India, though not so easily in Pakistan. Porter wages in Pakistan have risen twenty-fold since 1938, ten-fold since 1953.

EQUIPMENT

In 1938 we relied on woolen underwear, sweaters, and shirts, plus heavy windproof parkas. We had heavy wool socks and leather boots with tricouni nails, and specially knitted mittens with canvas shells. Down sleeping bags came from Switzerland or England. Tents came from the U.S., with some from Britain, and some left over from the 1936 Nanda Devi trip. We had only a few ice and rock pitons—real dinosaurs—but no karabiners or jumars. We used hemp ropes, long ice axes, and Crookes glass goggles of curious shape and color. Not much was given to us, and equipment cost $2,600, not including some items such as crampons (climbing irons fitted over boots) which each climber already had.

By 1953 equipment had changed dramatically. We still used a lot of wool, but down parkas (Karakoram model) were specially made to our design and donated to us by Eddie Bauer. Down sleeping bags were much improved, but costly. We took lightweight windproof shells to wear over wool sweaters and shirts. We had double leather boots with Bramani soles. Tents were lighter and better in 1953, but most of ours were leftovers from 1938. The only new one tore during the storm at Camp

VIII. We used nylon rope (which probably saved our lives because of its elasticity), but, as in 1938, we had few pitons and karabiners and no jumars. We did have three radios for communicating between camps. Oxygen and oxygen breathing equipment were expensive and heavy so we had only a small amount for use in a medical emergency. We used less than 500 feet of fixed rope. In 1953 our equipment cost approximately $4,300.

Today all equipment is lighter, carefully crafted, but horrendously expensive. Clothing is beautifully tough, colorful, and warm. Boots are much warmer. New types of crampons make climbing steep ice and snow much easier. Fixed rope by the mile, scores of pitons, and similar devices make possible speedy, often solo trips up and down a well-used route. Climbing ropes are of braided nylon and very strong. Tents are lighter, roomier, tougher. Stoves are lighter, more efficient, and less likely to explode. Much equipment can be wangled from manufacturers, greatly reducing the cost of an expedition, although each item is far more costly than in 1953. Expeditions tend to be smaller.

FOOD

Like an army, expeditions "travel on their stomachs," and food is of great interest to every person; many of them have specific preferences. For both expeditions we weighed and bagged individual items before starting, as we had learned from Brad Washburn. A larger bag had food for two men for one day; three of these in a tough outer bag provided everything for two men for three days, and weighed 18 pounds.

In 1938 we took a great variety of food. Breakfast was some type of easily cooked hot cereal, tea, and often dried fruit. Lunch consisted of crackers, cheese or sardines or tinned meat, and chocolate. For dinner, there were meats like Danish pemmican, fish, chicken, or hash, with home-dried vegetables, fruit, and tea. In our packs we also carried sugary snacks, malted milk tablets, and dried fruits. Our porters carried their own food, consisting mainly of flour and roasted barley. On the mountain our Sherpas ate much of what we ate. Our food cost $400, plus perhaps $100 for porter food.

For 1953 we followed much the same pattern. There were a few new items like dehydrated steak (in place of pemmican), compressed date and almond bars, Italian fruitcake, more dried vegetables, and more varieties of meat and fish. We took a little coffee, but preferred tea, as we had in 1938. Our food cost $1,200, and some was donated to us.

Today, food is different still, and much of it is freeze-dried. Each expedition has its own style and tastes. Food is costly, but commercialization is pervasive here as in the case of equipment. Many parties are given much of their equipment and food in exchange for endorsements.

Funding an expedition is always a problem, but it was more difficult in 1938, before commercial interests seized on the glamour of mountain expeditions. Each one of us contributed a share, and friends made up the rest. We were able to pay back a large loan by lectures and articles. The entire expedition in 1938 cost less than $9,500. In 1953, besides money from each of us and from friends, we received advances from the *Saturday Evening Post* and the National Broadcasting Company. Soon after our return we were able to quickly pay back a large loan. Income continued for several years, half of each payment given to the person who earned it and half divided among the others. The total cost of the expedition came to $31,000.

The whole scene is different today. The Himalayan countries charge high fees for attempting the great peaks. Many climbers are professionals. Television, lectures, books, sponsors, and endorsements are often lucrative. Being a professional guide on a big mountain can be quite profitable today.

HEALTH

In 1938 malaria, polio, dysentery, cholera, and smallpox were serious problems for which only symptomatic treatment was available. Immunizations against the last two were essential and required for international travel. As a fledgling medical student

I was stunningly ignorant of the health problems I might have to deal with; our medical kit was absurdly inadequate. As it turned out, bad blisters, group gastroenteritis from an orgy of overeating, and one fearsome case of dengue fever were all we had. Were we lucky, or did our precautions in food and drink, and our conservative climbing, protect us? In those days "the leader does not fall" was a universal precept, and a serious accident or death was not a sign of boldness but of poor judgment.

By 1953 a bewildering number of effective medicines had become available, notably the antibiotics and steroids, both expensive, and essential (we thought). I had become aware of the many medical mishaps which might befall us. Risk-taking had increased, and with this the number of accidents. We had only a little oxygen for emergencies. Altitude illnesses (discussed below) were poorly understood.

Today, a medical kit can and unfortunately must be extensive because of the potential for litigation. Furthermore, climbs and routes have become more extreme and are often done in frightful weather or at night. Accidents have become more frequent and more serious, and expedition doctors have faced desperate situations, and often won.

So powerful has been the drive to reach the summit that it overrides discretion. All too often those who have driven themselves too far have been weakened, enfeebled, and lost on the descent. Great ethical and philosophical questions have been added to the surgical and medical quandaries.

SPECIAL ALTITUDE PROBLEMS
Lack of oxygen

At high altitude lack of oxygen disturbs sleep, and saps appetite and strength. Above 22,000 feet deterioration outstrips acclimatization, and the climber who stays there for long grows weaker rather than stronger. More dangerously and very subtly, altitude weakens the higher centers of the brain, dulling judgment and perception. The climber high on K2 or Everest is like a sick man walking in a dream, making late or imperfect decisions which compound the risks. Now that all the highest summits are frequently reached without supplementary oxygen, many accidents may be due to the weakening of body and mind. Altitude illnesses are more frequent and more serious. The question of lasting brain damage has been raised but not resolved.

Frostbite

At great altitudes the dry cold air sucks heat and moisture from lungs and skin. Hypothermia drains will power. Cold reduces blood flow to the skin, especially to hands and feet. Lack of oxygen further increases susceptibility of fingers and toes to freezing. Throughout the centuries men on mountains have suffered frostbite and devised many different ways to treat frozen extremities. In 1953 we did not accept the painful injections and early amputation used for Maurice Herzog on Annapurna. Instead I elected to cleanse and dress Bell's blackened toes and fingers daily, keeping them sterile and dry; months later he lost only small bits of two toes.

The blood clots (thrombophlebitis) which led to Gilkey's death were a complication of thickened blood (from acclimatization), inactivity during the storm, and dehydration. The problem is not rare but was then unknown among mountaineers. However, even in hospital, treatment is often not helpful; in our situation I could do nothing to save him.

During our ten days imprisoned by storm at 25,000 feet we grew weaker and weaker. The wind kept us from restful sleep and we became more dehydrated and exhausted. Undoubtedly our judgment was warped by these combined stresses. Yet over and over again we weighed our few options carefully, without heroics, posturing, or self-serving. We always reached the same decision: when the storm abated we would get Art down or die trying to do so.

Thirty-three years later, during the same week in August, in almost the same place, seven men and women from four countries were trapped by a similar storm. Though they were some of the best climbers in the world, they too were drained by cold, and lack of oxygen, water, sleep, and food. They were hampered by different languages, and by differences in motivation and in their traditions of mountain ethics. In the end two saved themselves, leaving five to die in their tents or during the descent.

Brotherhood! No word said can make you brothers!
Brotherhood only the brave earn and by danger or
Harm or by bearing hurt and by no other

Archibald MacLeish
From "Speech to Those Who Say Comrade"

3 *The Tapes*

IN AUGUST, 1978, we met in the Wind River range in Wyoming to celebrate the twenty-fifth anniversary of our expedition to K2. Dee Molenaar thoughtfully brought along to our reunion the tape recordings we had made at Base Camp on August 16, the night we were all down safely off the mountain—all except Art Gilkey, that is. One evening around the campfire we played the tapes on Dee's portable recorder and talked about them, first hesitantly, and then with a rush. Though we each had a copy and had probably listened to them now and then, this was the first time we had listened together and had a chance to compare notes and clear up hazy memories. Although the emotion in our weary voices against a background of gusting winds and buzzing Coleman lantern is missing from the written word, the words are also powerful. Reproduced here, unedited save for a rare grammatical correction, is the tape we made that night, way back in 1953.

HOUSTON: It's August sixteenth, and our badly battered expedition is down here again, and we're going to talk over the events of the last three weeks, which have consisted almost entirely of storm. We left Camp III after a two-day storm, optimistically, and worked our way up to Camp IV, which we established. We climbed the famous House's Chimney and established Camp V, where we were again battered by another two-day storm. From then on, life seems to have been a continual series of winds, storms, snows, and other disasters. Bob Bates, you and Pete reconnoitered from Camp V to VI. What did you think about that route and the weather? And what do you think about the circumstances that accompanied us from then on?

BATES: Well, from V to VI we noticed that it was snowing, snowing lightly, and it took us quite a little while to find a good route. As a matter of fact, we would try first one side of the ridge and then another in an attempt to find something easy we could pack over. It was not a terribly long route, but it was one that caused us considerable anxiety because of the snow on the rocks. But we finally saw two tent poles sticking out against a black rock buttress above us. We were very pleased, we thought we'd be there in a few minutes, but it took us quite a while to huff up to it, and there we found something I will never forget. We found the remains of two camps with three sleeping bags and a primus stove, three packs all made up, all ready to go. These were the packs that the Sherpas had used 15 years ago when they had attempted to bring Dudley Wolfe down from the Camp VII of the Wiessner Expedition. The three men went up, attempting to bring him down, and never returned. What happened to them, we don't know. There was evidence that they were all set to return, and that they had expected to be gone not very long. Pete, was there anything else on the reconnaissance that you remember?

SCHOENING: No.

BATES: Nothing special. Well, from then on the plan was to pack up from Camp V to Camp VI, and that was done in fairly bad weather. Camp VI was established, and from Camp VI on the reconnaissance was made by Charlie, Bob Craig, and George. George, you remember that reconnaissance?

BELL: I remember it. We went up to Camp VI in the morning and got tents set up. That was a noteworthy afternoon; there was no wind; it was warm. The route-finding was a little tricky and we were certainly grateful for the good weather conditions.

And if I recall, that was about the best afternoon for the next three weeks, or something like that. We really couldn't call it very good, because it was overcast and there was no blue sky.

HOUSTON: What day was that?

BELL: Beats me.

HOUSTON: Anybody remember the day? Twenty-sixth? Twenty-seventh? Or twenty-eighth of July. That could be said to be our last good weather, right?

BELL: It was just one afternoon. After some storms, and high winds, and so forth, and before more. I guess, Charlie, you remember the next day rather vividly.

HOUSTON: We came back about six that afternoon, fairly bushed, and the next day we made a full-scale reconnaissance up to what we were going to call Camp VII. Do you remember how you hated that gully from VI to VII? Well, it certainly was as bad as anything you remember. Slabby, very steep, lots of ice and snow. The weather was bad; it got windy, cold, snowy, and that was the day that I came to grief and got thoroughly chilled, frosted my feet quite badly, but not too badly, and came back to camp to find the entire party assembled at Camp VI. That, I think, could be said to be the beginning of the bad weather that we had. July twenty-seventh. What do you think about the reconnaissance, Bob?

CRAIG: Well, I was struck by the difficulty of carrying loads up over the terrain. I think even in good weather it would be the sort of terrain that would require good porters, not average porters or persons who had little experience. It requires a lot of judgment, and unfortunately we didn't have as much fixed rope as we probably needed. But I think the biggest thrill of the reconnaissance team for George and me came when we went up and saw the ice slope that we had seen in pictures before and heard so much about, and we were very much impressed. It's a very smooth, hard stretch of ice and it's quite a formidable obstacle. But I think above all we were terribly worried about Charlie's frostbiting his feet that day; that's the thing that stands out in my mind. It was a cold, biting day when we went all the way up to Camp VII.

HOUSTON: Now, the next day was the twenty-eighth of July. What happened then?

MOLENAAR: Well, I have it in my journal that the next day Craig started to pack to Camp VII, and we only got as far as what we called the cache, the lower cache. It was a very cold day, and the wind was blowing quite hard, and a lot of us were fearful of frostbite, and I think two or three did get pretty badly chilled, and by the time they got back to Camp IV, they were very cold. Do you remember that day, remember when we were trying to get up that little section of fixed rope, and it was ice over rock?

CRAIG: I remember it was very, very cold there, and windy, and there was danger of rockfall, especially with eight men on one steep pitch of cliff with loose rock. It's very difficult to keep the top man from kicking off rocks that would hit the bottom man. As I recall, Tony was hit on the head that particular day.

STREATHER: Yes, I got hit quite hard on the head once.

CRAIG: It was snowing hard, wasn't it. Yes, as I recall, a very mean day.

HOUSTON: As I recall, a big rock came off and very nearly missed four or five of you. Just went right between you.

STREATHER: It exploded up between us, it hit hard, between Bob Bates and me, and went off with a hell of a bang.

HOUSTON: Well, anyway, we dumped our loads at the camp that day, and came back to VI, a little discouraged because we hadn't found a place for VII, right? The next day we took a party up determined to establish Camp VII, right? Pete and I, correct? Pete, do you remember that day?

SCHOENING: Yes, I think the idea was that Art and I were going to pack very light, just taking our personal gear—pack light, go fast, establish Camp VII, and then the remainder of the party would come up later in the day and back us up and help us to establish a very solid Camp VII. We got up to the ice slope in something like three or four hours, which is quite fast. From the ice slope, the old Camp VII from the previous attempt on the mountain, there was a traverse of the ice slope. We hoped to establish Camp VII over to a sérac field where we'd get protection from avalanches and so forth. From information we got from Bob Craig, we decided it might be better to go up the ice slope and then over to the séracs. We did work up this ice slope, probably about 200 or 300 feet high, cutting steps and using ice pitons. Above the top of the ice slope we ran into a snowfield. We placed a piton anchor at the top of the ice slope and then continued on up to about 150 feet or 200 feet higher. The weather was cloudy, or semi-cloudy, and so we couldn't see too much, but we did see the remainder of the party coming from below, so we decided to descend and get together with the rest of the party and see what would be the best thing to do. Up to this time, we had not been able to find the site of the old Camp VII, which was among the séracs. Charlie, you can tell what happened after we came back down and met the rest of the party. I remember this day was also very cold, very windy, there might have been some snow falling, I'm not too sure about that.

HOUSTON: I'll never forget that day. We got up there through driving clouds. I think it was snowing lightly, it was very cold and very windy. We saw you coming down what looked like a vertical cliff, and we saw no place for Camp VII at all. I remember feeling, personally, extremely desperate about what we were going to do. We had you-all pretty well committed to stay there. We didn't want to go back to VI, and I remember searching desperately for any place that was flat enough to put a tent, and when I say flat enough to put a tent I mean anything that might be three feet wide and six feet long. We were just about to give up, as I remember—isn't that correct?—and go back to the cache, when Bob Craig dug his ax into the snow in one particular place and found what amounted to a cave, and we were able to dig a shelf there, which was just about three feet wide and six feet long, where we pitched your tent. And I remember leaving you with a sinking heart because it was so bloody up there: cold, snowy, your tent platform negligible. The slope fell away very steeply below you, and we all knew that above you was a very steep slope such that if new snow fell it would be an avalanche slope, and might very well overcome you. Anyway, we went back to VI that night, and the next day planned to come back and rescue you, or at least to move up to help you. And the next day, as I remember, it was very stormy at Camp VI. Fortunately, we had radio contact with you and found that it wasn't quite as bad up where you were as it was at Camp VI. At VI we spent a quiet day in the tents. The wind was terrific. Six of us got into one tent, talking off and on, and while we were sitting in the tent together, Pete, you and Art were really doing Trojan work, and I'm particularly interested in what you found when you crossed the famous ice traverse of 1938 and looked for Camp VII on the other side.

SCHOENING: Well, a little while ago, Charlie, you mentioned that the storm wasn't raging up where we were, which might be called our Camp VII. It was blowing pretty hard, but we were in a position where if it did start to snow we were in a potentially bad avalanche spot, so we had to move. I remember that morning it was quite windy in camp, but the tent was protected by a slight ridge. Our plan now was to find a safer Camp VII, and consequently we decided to make the traverse and find the old Camp VII of the 1938–1939 expedition. By going about 100 feet or 200 feet from where our tent was pitched, we went around more or less to the east, and very luckily got away from the wind. We sort of got behind this little ridge or around a buttress, and consequently in making the traverse we were in no wind, although it was quite cold. I remember the climbing was not too tough. We could kick steps in some of the places, had to chop them in others. At any rate, the belays were quite lengthy; I remember one belay I sat for about an hour, which if you're in very much of a wind can chill down the body regardless of how much clothing you have on. Incidentally, we had on every bit of clothing we had up there at the camp at the time. We did make this traverse and got over to what looked like some séracs. However, it was more or less an ice wall. Beyond and below the ice wall was nothing but a snow slope. It looked or seemed almost like a wind slab slope. It was quite steep, I suppose maybe about 35 degrees, which isn't really steep as far as snow slopes go, but too steep to pitch a tent on, and it was also an avalanche slope. This day was sort of spottedly cloudy; we could see maybe 100 yards and then the clouds would blow away. We saw nothing that would resemble a campsite. We concluded from this that there'd been quite a change from 1938 and 1939, and that the previous campsite had been obliterated by either a large avalanche or just a slow change in snow conditions in that area.

During this time we had radio contact with Colonel Ata-UIlah down in Base Camp, but not with you at Camp VI because your radio was not transmitting, although it was receiving. After finding this development we returned to our precariously pitched little tent and decided that we'd better follow the steps we'd made the day before and go up the ice slope and see what we could find up on top. We thought maybe we'd be able to dig into a ridge someplace. A ridge would be safe from avalanches anyway. We did work up the ice slope, using the anchor we'd made the day before, for two rope lengths and continued on up this snow slope, which again we analyzed as an avalanche slope. It was ankle- to knee-deep snow. After running out two rope lengths we continued on, leaving our piton anchor, of course, and worked on up the slope for possibly seven or eight rope lengths. In elevation it'd be about 400 feet, I suppose. All this time we couldn't see much of the mountain; the clouds were quite thick, except when wind blowing by would just give us enough leeway to keep on going and know that we weren't getting ourselves in a very precarious position. After a while, we did reach the top of what you might call a ridge—it would actually be the shoulder of K2—and found a very good campsite protected from avalanches, and a nice level spot, plenty of room for tents. This was definitely right on the shoulder. We dumped our loads, light loads, probably about 20 pounds, and returned to our previous Camp VII, the one that's sort of pitched on a little ledge chopped in the snow right at the edge of the rocks, and reported our findings to you on the radio with the idea that on the following day we would continue up and establish this higher camp, which was eventually called Camp VIII. You want to add anything to that, Charlie?

HOUSTON: I've got nothing to say, except that it was a wonderful job you did that day. We were all filled with admiration for you, because the weather was such that we didn't want to go out of Camp VI. Now, the next day the weather was just about as bad, blowing, snowing, correct? Everybody remember that? We decided that we would try to go up anyway, because we felt we had to help Pete and Art move camp in order to get them established, and we wanted to get on up the mountain ourselves. By this time, as I remember, we were beginning to feel that if you didn't move in bad weather on this mountain, or at least in dubious weather, you wouldn't move at all. So, we went on up, reaching Camp VII—that miserable ledge camp— as I remember it, about noon, after a rather unpleasant trip, and we found Pete and Art just about ready to move up to Camp VIII. So we all packed up loads and in about three hours we arrived at Camp VIII. I for one was pretty bushed. There was very little wind, as I remember it, but big clouds and snow. We pitched the tents and climbed in about four o'clock in the afternoon of July thirty-first, or August first?

CRAIG: August first.

HOUSTON: We considered ourselves pretty happy and successful at getting to Camp VIII, which we reckoned as being between 25,500 and 25,300. The wind blew all that night.

CRAIG: Early in the evening it looked very nice, and then it started blowing.

HOUSTON: Then it started to blow, and it blew hard. The next day we had a beautiful sunrise, crystal-clear, warm, sunny. We thought, oh boy, this is the beginning of the good weather. We had good radio contact with Camp VI, with Bob and you, Tony, and the arrangement was that you were going to come up and meet us at Camp VII, or at the cache, provided the weather continued good. Tell us about your trip up.

STREATHER: Well, that morning, Charlie, was one of the best we'd had for quite a few days. The sun dawned quite bright, and Bob and I were full of cheer. We'd stayed down, you remember, the day before, and we were still in Camp VI, and we'd decided that we would come on up and join you that day. We arranged to meet you at the cache and then all join there and go on up to Camp VIII together. We got up early and soon after we started the weather started to go back to its normal miserable self, it started clouding over. However, we were quite determined then that we would come up; we'd already gotten ourselves ready. I think we both realized that if we didn't come up then, we'd probably never get any higher. We eventually left camp at about eight o'clock. The weather continued to deteriorate, and we very soon found that we were in for quite a difficult time, under pretty bad conditions. We continued to climb the rest of the morning and at about twelve o'clock, it must have been, we heard you up at the cache at VII and you were shouting something at us. It was very windy.

HOUSTON: We heard you shouting first.

STREATHER: You heard us shouting, did you? Well, we thought we heard you say that you were going back, going back to Camp VIII. But it might well have been, as it turned out later, that you were telling us to go back, because you thought the climb would be too long. But having gone all that distance, particularly having climbed over the difficult slabs, the steep slab rock between VI and the so-called VII, we thought that it would be easier to go on than it would to go back over these difficult slabs.

HOUSTON: The only reason we shouted was that the storm was so bad that we were afraid you'd get up above the cache and find no place to camp, and be unable to get on to VIII, so I thought it was safer for you to go back, so that's why we were so insistent on you going home, going down to VI.

CRAIG: I might say one thing: that is the coldest day that I remember working on the mountain outside of the tenth of

August, when we had our retreat from the mountain. It was a terribly cold day, and I know that Dee and I got back into Camp VIII with very, very cold feet and hands and I think a nip of frostbite.

STREATHER: Well, anyhow, I think once we got going we were determined to get up to Camp VIII. I remember we stopped and ate a little lunch and we both climbed into my bivouac sack to keep the wind off us and rested; that helped us quite a bit. We climbed and got to the cache campsite, so-called Camp VII, and we squatted there for a bit to put on our crampons, and then we set about following the route up the last part of the snow slope.

HOUSTON: I think that was the part that scared me, I didn't think you'd be able to find your way up that ice slope. Terribly steep slope, deep snow at the top, we knew it would be blowing, and I was afraid that, number one, if we waited for you we'd get frosted, and number two, if we didn't wait for you that day you'd never find your way to Camp VIII in spite of those willow wands that we put into the snow.

STREATHER: Well, the first steep part of the ice slope, we were able to see the route; you put in the willow wands and the fixed ropes. Art and Pete did a wonderful job on the fixed ropes and the step cutting, and we just followed up there. Then once we got above the fixed rope, you'd been very thoughtful in putting willow wands and we could just see from one to the other, and as we went slowly forward up the snow slope we could see one willow wand and then the next. Bob was leading and he did a really wonderful job. We went very, very slowly but eventually Bob turned around to me and said, "We're there," and in a few more steps we were up over the shoulder and into the camp in front of us. It had been a pretty hard day, and as far as I can remember we'd been climbing for nearly ten hours in a fairly consistent storm.

BATES: The first part of the route up from Camp VI was so covered with snow that it took us about three times as long as it normally would, and after two hours of climbing we'd been over slopes that we just didn't want to go back over, and we were just determined that if we possibly could we were going to make it up to VIII. I can't add anything else except that the wind never stopped all day and that the snow storming in one's face made it difficult to keep one's sense of direction, and use the holds that one should. We were very glad to be there at Camp VIII.

HOUSTON: Boy, were we glad to see you. I think we were all pretty surprised. Well, we were surprised in a way, but I had a feeling all afternoon that you were going to turn up. I was frankly a little upset that you had done it. Now this was on the second of August.

CRAIG: Surprised or not, we were all tremendously delighted to see you. All of us at 25,500 feet and in good condition, ready for the top.

BATES: And less than 3,000 feet to get to the summit.

HOUSTON: Well then, going to the next day—all of us were there. It blew like hell that night; it was furious. We were glad to be together, but we needed a break. The next morning was about as stormy as any day we'd had, I think. Nothing happened that day, except we lay in bed . . . [The tape is unintelligible here.]

HOUSTON: And you lie there in your sleeping bag, warm, with snow blowing in on you, the tent buffeting over your head, unable to cook, can't light the stove, can't melt snow for water, can't cook. It seems impossible to endure it, and it goes on and on and on and on. Now I'd say that one of the really bright spots of that week of storm was the fact that we communicated with you, Ata, over and over again morning and night, and could talk to you and get cheer from Base Camp. It just seemed as though we couldn't stand it otherwise. The only other thing I want to say about the storm is that George and I were in this impervious tent which isn't too bad, but during the night of August third the fabric of the tent split. It didn't actually tear, but the split grew wider and wider and we could see the light through the crack and finally about seven o'clock that morning the tent gave. We had a feeling all that night that should the tent go down we wouldn't stand a chance of surviving. We made up our minds to stay in the tent, even though it blew down, right? We couldn't get out. Because we decided if we did go out and put our boots and gloves on and go the ten feet to the other tent—six feet I guess it was—we thought we'd freeze to death before we got there. Well, it was a pretty bad night as I recall it, and in the morning when the tent finally gave, we had stayed in it for long enough to get our things on in the daylight and then we went over, each to another tent. I went in with you and Bob Bates, Tony. And George went in with Art and Pete. Three men in those little tents in a storm is no fun. Now what do you remember about the next day, Tony?

STREATHER: Well, Charlie, before you came into our tent, Bob and I had had on the first day of the storm quite a job trying to keep the thing down and from dragging away with both of us in it. When the storm was really at its strongest, the first day, we both huddled in one end with our shoulders against the end of the tent, so it would neither float a bit nor fly away with both of us in it. We eventually had a chance to get out in a slight lull to make the tent a little more secure with the ice axes we could find, and then on the day that your tent went, you came on in with us. Well, we were in the Swiss tent that had a liner, and the first night was terrible with three of us in the minute space under the silk liner. We very soon realized that the only good thing we could say about it was that it was dry, so the next day we took the liner off and just had the outer part of the tent, which made it much larger, but not as dry, and certainly not as warm. Well, the days just went on. Each evening we'd say, "Well, perhaps tomorrow will be better, and we'll get a break," but we never did. The wind just kept on and on and on and on blowing. The tent sides flapping against our heads and shoulders driving us crazy. But what was probably most important of all, the tent flapped so much that we couldn't cook because we couldn't keep a stove lighted. We could eat dried food, but we didn't have anything to drink, and at that altitude drink is absolutely essential to not becoming rapidly dehy-drated. I think as a doctor you'll tell us that our blood gets thicker and we feel the cold more.

HOUSTON: Now wait a minute, there's something very important that we forgot. About that day, somewhere near the day that George and I came in to you, we decided to select the summit team. Our hopes were really getting pretty high then. We thought, "Since we've had five days of storm we can't pos-sibly have any more storm." So, we did something which I think is unique to this expedition, something which I think we ought to be very proud of: we balloted for the summit team and we selected a first team and a second team. By choice of the entire expedition of those who were fittest and most likely to get to the top, we selected two teams. The first team was George and Pete. No, the first team was George and Bob Craig. The second team was Pete and Art. We had our plans made to move up to Camp IX. All of us would carry up to Camp IX. The first two would move up to Camp IX first, and then the next day the next team would do the same thing. I think for a Himalayan expedition that's an unusual way to choose a summit party—to have eight men at 25,000 feet in such good condition that we could—that we were not forced to, but found it desirable to—ballot to see who could go to the summit. I think that was very exciting. I remember Art Gilkey particularly was determined that all eight of us would get to the top if we had good weather. The rest of us were not quite so optimistic. Well, anyway, every night we went to bed thinking tomorrow's going to be the day, tomorrow we'll send the first team up, and tomorrow maybe they'll make a bid for the summit. And we were in a position to do that. And then all of a sudden the real blow came. What day was it that Art first complained about his leg? Do you remember, Bob? The seventh? The first day that Art complained about his leg was a real blow. The first indication that anything was wrong.

MOLENAAR: I think that Bob Craig and I were going up with Art to Camp VIII. Art was at the bottom end of the rope and he wanted to untie the rope because he couldn't keep up with us even at the slow pace we were going through the deep snow. That was probably the first indication that he had something wrong with his leg.

CRAIG: But we first knew about it really on the seventh when Art got up and he was walking over from the tent to Tony, and walking over in the snow there he had a fainting spell and fell in the snow momentarily, and Charlie went over and examined him. Isn't that the case, Charlie?

HOUSTON: It was a fairly warm morning. I wouldn't say it was a nice morning; it was cloudy and it was snowing, but it wasn't blowing. He fainted, and when he came to he said that he had a charley horse in his leg, and I examined him and found that he had blood clots in his left leg—thrombophlebitis—without any question at all. And I put him back into bed with a bandage on it, and then I came and told you-all that he was probably going to be unable to walk for some time. That was the first thing that showed us that we were coming close to disaster.

STREATHER: That was on the seventh, wasn't it, Charlie?

HOUSTON: The seventh. Now my memory gets a little hazy after that, but it seems to me that we had no choice, because the weather deteriorated again, and we had so much storm that we couldn't do much.

CRAIG: Didn't we make an attempt to haul him down by the main way? We tried to haul him down that day, but ran into extremely dangerous avalanche conditions.

HOUSTON: That was the first day without real storm and we tried to haul him down. We broke camp fairly completely, packed him up in a sleeping bag and tent, started down the slope, and got about 300 feet, or 200 feet, snow sometimes hip deep, sometimes knee deep, and very obviously it was an avalanche slope, and decided that we had to go back. So we brought him back—taking about an hour and a half to cover 200 feet. I know it was one of the most frightful skirmishes that we had. He tried hopping on one leg, then we'd jerk him up.

He'd hop, and we'd jerk. And then the only thing bright about that day was when Bob Craig and Pete decided to go down another route to see whether there was a way around this avalanche slope. Pete, tell us about that trip down, because that was really the thing that saved our lives. If you hadn't done that I don't think we'd be here.

SCHOENING: On the way up we'd come up the ice slope, and then up this potential avalanche slope. Our new route, which Art and I had noticed on a reconnoiter trip, was along the ridge. There was a rocky ridge that extended down and eventually ran into Camp VII. Bob and I followed this ridge down approximately 300 feet, whereupon it went off sort of an abrupt cliff, but at this cliff point it was possible for climbing members—or members that could climb—to climb down the rock, more or less down the cliff. It would be possible to evacuate a person by sliding him down the col, or snow groove, between the rocks and the snow slope, which was off to our left as we faced down. At the base of this cliff was an ice traverse of possibly 100 feet or 200 feet that ended up on the rock near where Camp VII was situated. Bob and I were just able to look over this route through the clouds which whisked by, and see that it was feasible, and then return back to Camp VIII. The fact that we did have a route that would get us down to Camp VII was quite a relief in our minds, and to that extent it was quite valuable.

HOUSTON: It was life-saving. It was the only thing that gave us an out. If we hadn't had that route that you and Bob found, we would have been absolutely licked there. We couldn't have come down that avalanche slope safely. That's an understatement, Pete. Then we took Art back and settled down in the tent—that would be the seventh still. On the eighth and the ninth we just sat there. More storm. Terrific storm. I don't think any of us have ever experienced a storm like that.

CRAIG: On the eighth it did calm down enough so that in the afternoon you sent two of us to go up, to see how far we could go up and look around and see where we were on the plateau. We did go up three or four hundred feet above Camp VIII, but we were in fog. We couldn't see more than a rope length ahead, climbing up the side of a broken-up part of the glacier—this plateau glacier, more or less an icefall—climbing on the right side of it, and I suppose we got to 26,000 feet, 25,800 feet, somewhere in there. Well, we couldn't see a thing, and we waited for twenty minutes in the fog. We were very apprehensive about Art by this time; we talked about the need for getting down, the fear of being stuck up there, the fact that people were getting tired, deteriorating, and then we came back to camp. We talked to Charlie and everyone seemed to have crystallized this feeling in his own mind at the same time.

HOUSTON: As you said, we decided that [inaudible] . . . and let him get well, and then all of a sudden, bang, the other leg became involved, and his lungs were involved. At that point it became obvious that if we were going to get him down alive, he had to go then. We were getting to the point then, ourselves, of being so weak, so dehydrated, and so undernourished, that if we didn't go down, we might not survive. Beginning about the seventh of August I felt that we were fighting for our own lives, as well as Art's, and that if we didn't start down pretty soon, none of us would survive. What did you think about that, Bob?

BATES: Well, for several days I'd been very concerned about the condition we were in, the amount of food, the fact that we were having so much difficulty cooking, that we couldn't get enough water, that we were all having cold feet, mainly because of dehydration, the fact that it took practically all night to warm up one's feet in a sleeping bag even though we were inside a tent. I was tremendously relieved when you announced that the best thing was to have two people stay up and wait until Art improved enough so that he could walk down. I was very concerned about the idea of trying to lower him down, we had such great difficulty on the seventh when we first tried it. The only thing that worried me was—if you and someone else stayed there—whether a support party would be able to come back with enough food and gas so that you would be absolutely safe. When you made the decision that we ought to take Art down, again I was worried because of the weather. It was a helluva day. It was blowing and storming. And yet when you told us that there was one chance of saving his life, there was absolutely no question but that it was the thing to do. What did you think yourself about that trip down on that day?

HOUSTON: Well, I'm no rescue expert. The rescue experts told me that we could get him down. As far as I was concerned it seemed to me about as desperate a thing to do as we could try. Pete, you were pretty optimistic about getting him down. How come?

SCHOENING: I'm optimistic about getting a person off a mountain, even a mountain with the terrain that we had to go over. I think Tony and Bob will back me up about the morning we had to leave—the tenth. The weather was frightful and making an evacuation in bad weather is really something terrific, and I expressed to both of them that I was really worried about that day because of the bad weather. Bob, you've done a little rescue work; what did you think of the situation that morning?

CRAIG: I shared your optimism when I started, except for the weather, and another thing that I don't think you or I realized, though it was in the back of Charlie and Bob's minds because they had been here before: that's a terrible thing called altitude and wind. I know, having reached you after bringing Art down through this snow and ice gully, myself being belayed by the others above, that I was finished, at least for an hour. I could hardly lift my arms I was so tired, so completely worn out, and so completely cold. I think that's where the danger to the men in the party lay. Seven men's lives were in the balance, along with the one life they were trying to save.

HOUSTON: Art was wrapped up in a sleeping bag and a tent, with gloves, socks, boots, and a little pillow under his head. I think he was fairly warm, he seemed comfortable, with a rope around his waist and under his arms, a double rope as I remember. We let him down that gully and held him there for a long time, and that's when the avalanche went over Bob Craig.

STREATHER: I remember that bit quite well, Charlie. You and Bates belayed very strongly on a rope, and Bob Craig went down with Art and I remember I was a little way down so I could shout to you and shout to them, because the wind was so strong that they couldn't hear, even though they were only a rope's length away. I remember the rope suddenly cut through the snow and started off quite a large avalanche. I shouted down to Bob Craig, but he didn't hear. Fortunately, he hung on tight just below us, and I remember very clearly seeing the two of them just disappear as the snow went down through this very narrow gully, over their heads. As the snow cleared I was very relieved and a little surprised to see them both still there. From then on Bob Craig was pretty well waxed; that was about the last thing which really sapped the strength out of him. I remember shouting up from the bottom, "Hold him ! He's on the edge of a cliff."

HOUSTON: Oh my God, I'll never forget that: "Hold him! He's on the edge of a cliff."

STREATHER: You were just holding on, freezing up at the top there. Pete and Dee had gone on ahead, and then I think I saw Pete come up to Bob and secure him—no, I think it was Dee—to eventually pull him across the ice slope.

CRAIG: One thing I think we shouldn't forget here is that— at least while I was going down with Art—George Bell, who had frostbitten feet to begin with, was in a belay position up above all the time and gave one of the soundest belays that you could possibly want to both Art and me, and I think that George jeopardized his feet a tremendous amount, both in this particular operation and later on.

HOUSTON: Well, from there on my memory is gone.

BATES: Well, after that you and I both climbed down, and George—down the rocky cliff—and Tony—I guess the four of us—and reached Pete, who was belaying Art, who was just below a short but very steep cliff. Tony at that point climbed down to Art to see if he could help him, and anchor him, and see if he could help work him across to Camp VII.

STREATHER: Yes, as far as I can remember after we got down through that narrow gully, Pete and you and Charlie belayed Art down a very steep cliff, and George Bell belayed me and I went down with Art. I remember it was so steep that the ropes which were around him kept catching on little bits of rock. I remember once he got completely caught, and I shouted up to you to try to pull him up a bit. I kicked off the ropes and eventually he slipped down. You lowered him down the cliff, and George lowered me down, and we got just onto the ice slope below the cliff. Well, that was the last ice slope and it leads across to Camp VII. As we looked down we were on the right of it, and we had to pull Art and get ourselves across about 150 feet to the left to where the ledge from Camp VII would be. Well, it was just about here that the accident really happened. I remember there was a double white rope to Art, and having gone down with him, I made sure this was secure, had a last word with him, and then got across the ice slope to where you and Charlie had come down. We then had a double white rope to pull Art across the ice slope, and Pete was belaying him still from the original rope above the cliff. George, at that stage, was still up top; he stopped belaying me and started to climb over to join us. Well, George had been having a very bad time; he'd already been frozen fairly badly, and the extra time waiting at the top there seemed to have frozen him even more, and I remember looking up and seeing him climb across, but his hands seemed more like clubs; they didn't seem to be very effective. I remember seeing him appear to take a handhold and then begin to slip; I can't remember who it was that shouted, but suddenly he was sliding and going very fast down this very steep ice slope. I could see that he was trying very hard to arrest himself, but his hands didn't seem to be effective, and he just didn't stop himself. He was still tied to me, and we weren't tied to anyone else. George went past me going fast and I tried hard to get my belay firmer, but we were on a pretty steep slope and all we had was an ice ax driven partly into the ice, and our crampons. Well, as soon as the rope tightened I was whipped off the slope like a fly. I remember quite clearly everything that happened from then on. I went off and I fell quite a ways trying to arrest myself, but it seemed to have no effect at all. After a few seconds of falling there was a very sudden jerk and I stopped just momentarily, and that must have been when George's and my rope crossed the double white rope from Art. And you, Bob Bates, and Charlie were both onto that, and so was Dee. I can't remember how everyone was tied. That second jerk meant the rest of you three were falling. I fell again, possibly another 50 feet, quite helpless, there was nothing I could do about it. Suddenly there was another jerk and I stopped. There seemed to have been three successive tugs around my stomach and miraculously we had all stopped. I think what happened is that George's rope and my rope must have crossed the rope to which Art was anchored: that stopped George and me. At the same time I crossed your ropes and pulled the three of you off at the same time. When I finally finished falling there were about a hundred ropes around my stomach, and yours had somehow caught around me, and somehow miraculously we all held; we were all held by Pete, who had a very, very good belay on Art, who was way, way above us by then, about 200 feet above us. I think it was really remarkable that Pete was able to hold all five of us. I think we ought to mention that if Pete hadn't done that remarkable job he would have been pulled off himself, and Art would have gone, and we would have all gone, except for Bob Craig, who was unroped. I remember then trying to look around, and I saw George just appearing out of a little gully. He slowly started to climb again after the fall. I didn't see you other three. You'd all disappeared over a rocky cliff, and I didn't know who was there. I remember standing to my feet and moving slightly forward, and then eventually after the chaos, Charlie, you and Bob and Dee climbed up from the rocky ice cliff down behind me on the right, and George started climbing up from the very bottom. He must have fallen 250, 300 feet, a full rope length above and a full length below me. I think Bob Bates was then probably in a better position to see what went on after that.

BATES: I saw Tony swept off the slope as if by a giant hand, and Charlie a fraction of a second later, and the next thing I knew I was flipped over backwards, and went bump, bump over rock ledges, sure that this was the end, there wasn't a chance that anything could hold us, and by a miracle, just when I thought the next big bump was going to be 150 feet or more, it stopped. I stopped with my hands tied up in the rope, head-first, backward, down the slope, apparently right on the edge of something, and just by a miracle I heard a voice above me, and somebody said, "Who's there?" and I said, "It's Bob," and it was Dee, and he released me. When I started to my feet I saw George coming up from below—George, who had been 100 feet above us before, was now 75 feet below me, with his hands white, saying, "My hands are freezing." Down below me was a figure which I figured out was Charlie, unconscious. Dee was beside me, and above me I could see Tony struggling to his feet and moving around. As soon as George got a little closer, I went down and gave him a spare pair of Indian mittens which I happened to have in my pocket, and then unroped and went down to Charlie Houston, who was unconscious. I shook him; he came to, but he didn't know where he was. He kept asking what had happened, and where he was, and what he was doing there, and I got him to climb up a very steep 15 feet or more to Dee, who was belaying him. I climbed up after him and went over to the tiny tent platform of Camp VII, to see if we could get some kind of shelter from the raging blizzard where Bob Craig had been working. Bob took Charlie over to the tent platform, and the couple worked on the tent there and finally got it up. George came over, and pretty soon the whole group of us was there, either working on the tent, or working on another platform for a bivouac tent which would be able to shelter the whole party from the elements. We were all terribly weak, and almost everyone had some trouble. Dee had a cracked rib, Charlie had a concussion and a bad rib. Bob had been pretty well exhausted from the previous effort, and Pete had trouble with his chest; also for a while he had terribly cold hands. By the time we had the two tents up, we'd probably been away from Art for forty-five minutes, or possibly an hour. Before Craig had come down to help us, we had gone over and anchored Art very securely; Tony had also put a belay on Art, so that there were two very strong ice ax belays on him. Bob had also told Art a little of what had happened, and he had told Art that he would come back as soon as the injured from the fall had been taken care of. About an hour elapsed between the time that Bob had told him this and the time when three of us went back to see if we could move him. When we came back to the slope, which is only about 200 feet from where we were working—about 150 feet—to our amazement, the slope was bare! We don't know what happened, but probably an avalanche had come down and swept Art and the ice axes and everything off the slope. We never heard it, we never saw it, but when we came back, 150 feet from where we were working, the slope was bare and Art was gone. It was just as if the hand of God had swept him away.

HOUSTON: Didn't Tony see something there?

STREATHER: Well, we went back to do something with Art. What we had in mind was making a little ledge in the slope and resting him there for the night, covering him up and resting him. We realized that the three of us, all very weak, would be unable to drag him over to VII, and the rest of the party at that time were in even worse state than ourselves. We got to the slope, and Bob said, "There." Now most of the day we'd been working without goggles because the goggles just fogged up. And I know that I and Bob Bates were both going a little blind. Bob, I remember, went first and said, "Art's gone," and I went right on past Bob, he gave me a belay, and I went right out onto the slope where Art had been. The whole thing to me looked different. My eyes were hazy, but I'm sure that through the haze I saw a peculiar groove right down the middle of the slope and somehow the rest of the snow looked different. It was a different texture. I remember seeing a rock at the top of the groove, and the first thought that went through my head is that there'd been an avalanche and Art had been swept clean with the slope. That was the impression I got through a very hazy, exhausted look at the slope. We came back to Camp VII, where we bivouacked for the night.

BATES: When we got back there, four of us got into a very, very small tent which we'd had on the main slope, and three of us got into the bivouac tent, on the other little ledge. There was just room to sit shoulder-to-shoulder and try not to let our feet go over the side. The tent billowed dangerously because the ledge was so narrow that the tent overhung the ledge, and we couldn't nail the tent onto the slope very well because of the nature of the ice. There was a great danger all night long that if we leaned a little bit forward the whole tent with everybody in it would go down. It was a long, very, very tedious night. Charlie was out of his head and kept wanting oxygen and to cut a hole in the top of the tent. The three in the bivouac tent were miraculously able to get a stove going and cook some tea and hand out cups to the other tent. All seven managed to get through the night. Thank God it was a windless night, the first windless night we'd had in weeks, and the first break that the weather had given us in a long, long time. Next morning we got up and were able to eat a little food and get started down to Camp VI. We knew we had to get down, we had very little gas and food and we had to get down to a real camp. Bob, would you like to talk a bit about that trip down? It was a helluva morning as I remember it.

CRAIG: Charlie was beginning to come around again, so Charlie, Pete, and myself climbed on one rope, and I remember Bob Bates, Tony, George, and Dee climbed on the other rope. I must say that Charlie, having had a very severe concussion and a very painful injury to his chest, climbed down very nicely and gave really strong belays, although most of our climbing didn't depend so much on belays as on just staying on our feet, and not falling. It was icy, snowy, and very, very bitterly cold climbing down. When we finally arrived down at VI in mid-afternoon and started digging out the tents there, which had been collapsed after this continuous snowfall of the last four weeks of storm and wind, some of the guy ropes were down. We got things ready and the second rope finally came in. When they got in, everyone was bitterly cold, chilled right through to the bone, and we had quite a problem warming up. Then began, I think, one of the most desperate parts of the trip. We were by no means out of danger. The trip from VII to VI was a most important one, but from VI on down we began quite a fight. I think George Bell is one of the most important people in that fight because he showed remarkable courage in coming down with frostbitten feet, badly frostbitten, climbing beautifully down over ice-covered rock all the way. The mountain fought us all the way down to Camp II, where we finally began to feel that we were safe. George, what do you think about the trip below?

BELL: Well, it was a pretty hideous descent. The weather never let up and the route was entirely different from the first ascent, but we knew we had to get down because there were no great reserves of food or fuel above, and we were getting weaker by the day. So it was just a job that had to be done, and was done.

HOUSTON: The thing I remember best about the descent—the thing I remember worst about the descent—is that we just never had any surcease from the wind and the snow, we never had enough strength, we never had anything to drink. Remember mixing up that jam with snow? You lived in a tent with a hole in it, you were covered with snow, you were all cold, our sleeping bags were wet, we had insufficient everything, two sleeping bags had been lost, we'd lost our cooking pots, we'd lost one radio, we'd lost our stove, and we had to get down because, first of all, we were short on fuel and food, and secondly because of the condition of George's feet, and the fact that the rest of our feet were getting pretty bad. The one thing I remember right at Camp VIII was the contact that we had had with Ata at Base Camp. It was cheery for us at night and in the morning, and it was enough to give us a lot of courage—then thirty-six hours without radio contact with us, at which he was as desperate for news of us as we were for getting down to Base Camp. That was after the radio had been lost, and before we got down to Camp VI. I don't know how we got from VI to V. That was really in some way the worst day of all, but we did get there. And when we did get to V somehow we managed to get down House's Chimney, the last part of it in the dark. Then we got down to IV, and through IV. The next day we went down to III, and the weather was very much the same. The route from IV to III, I remember as being particularly unpleasant. When we got down to III we tried to decide whether to go down to II that afternoon, for we'd been climbing about six hours already. We had to decide whether to go down in our weakened condition or make a bivouac there. I think we decided correctly in going down. And then came one of the great experiences of the whole trip. Remember when we got close down to Camp II—we heard the Hunzas shouting and we shouted to them. We arrived at Camp II just at dark—we must have been climbing about ten hours—close to exhaustion. And we were greeted by our Hunzas, who came rushing up, tied together with little quarter-inch ropes, and threw their arms around us, burst into tears. They had prayers, sobbing, shouting. Go on from there, Bob.

CRAIG: Well, I can't describe it except to say that it's the deepest experience I've ever had with a human being. The Hunzas came up to meet us in groups as we came in by ropes. The first rope included Charlie, who did this marvelous job of leading us down from Camp III through very difficult ice-covered rock. They took our packs off our backs on traverses that were slopes of 40 degrees, in the one case. Just took our packs off our backs, and embraced us and cried on us, and then when we got into camp we were so overcome by this display of emotion and feeling and warmth that we just didn't know what to say or what to do, we were all in. They brought us hot rice and milk and tea and hot parattas, the national biscuit of Pakistan, and they completely surrounded us, rubbing our legs and giving us the most thoughtful care, taking care of every possible need. That night it was just something. They gathered together, we told them about Art, Tony explained to them in Urdu what had happened above, how we just barely got down, and then a very spontaneous and I think a very touching prayer was led by Kairal Hidayat. It was the first time we really had a chance to express our feelings all together. Then to bed; we were completely exhausted. The next morning we were waked up finally and had breakfast, more feelings were expressed, and then on down to Base Camp we started. By this time George's feet were very bad, pretty severe frostbite, so carefully roped we started down.

[Here the 1953 tape ends.]

Here the tape ran out and our thoughts turned to those no longer with us. Art Gilkey, our friend whose death we had tried so hard to prevent but in vain. Ata-Ullah, who had strengthened us in so many ways during times of desperation. We talked about them almost as if they had been with us, and we talked too about Bill House, who had been such a strong member of the 1938 party and had patiently served as our treasurer in 1953, but was unable to share the reunion with us. We talked about many adventures in many places, but we came back again and again to the days of trial at Camp VIII and during the nightmare descent, trying to fill in gaps in our sometimes varying memories. So much of the expedition was as fresh as yesterday, and so much was clouded by the pain and sorrow that climaxed all.

HOUSTON: Listening to our voices on those tapes makes me realize how close to complete exhaustion we were when we got down. The nightmare at Camp VIII was still blurred, at least for me. For example, I've thought for years that Art's phlebitis began about the third rather than the seventh of August, and that we had many days of worry and uncertainty. I remember talking with Ata many, many times—not that he could do much except send us courage. I knew, but could not tell the rest of you, that Art's chances of survival were almost zero under those rugged conditions. We had very few options: we could all stay at VIII until Art got better, or died, or until we all died. Or we could leave Art and save ourselves while we still had strength, but no one even considered this. Or one or two people could stay with him while the others went down, recovered, and came back for us. Obviously, as the doctor in the party, I would stay with him, and all the others offered to stay with me, but should anyone else? Or we could try to haul and carry him down that rocky, almost unknown ridge that ended in the cliff above Camp VII—difficult enough in good weather, but I thought impossible in storm. None of these choices was very appetizing. Ever since then it has seemed to me that we agonized for many, many days, not just for three. I can't listen to that recording without great feeling—there's so much in it and so much we didn't say. Meeting Ata-Ullah on the glacier, the loving welcome at Camp II and again at Base, where there was space to move about, and water—all the water we could drink. Unforgettable memories. I was still very shaky at Base and had trouble moving my head. I couldn't read the service for Art, near that splendid cairn the porters built a day or two later. Do you remember that, Bob?

BATES: I certainly do. We were still so tired that climbing the short slope to the cairn was a major effort. Our battered group stood there with bowed heads, perhaps each of us thinking, "Why Art and not me?" It was a moving though simple service.

HOUSTON: Our Hunza porters were very moved. The whole little party had grown very close. Then the Balti porters came in, on schedule, on August sixteenth and we packed up and left next day, carrying George on an improvised stretcher. How much of that do you remember, George?

BELL: Riding on the stretcher wasn't very memorable, especially since the weather continued foul and there weren't even any good views. But I will never forget being carried on the back of Mohammed Hussein and the other Satpura porters for all the toughest miles. I particularly remember peering over Mohammed Hussein's shoulders and watching his great bare feet carrying both of us from one sharp boulder to the next, with no hesitation and perfect balance. Also, the first fruit and fresh vegetables in Askole and beyond seemed the best in the world.

HOUSTON: And finally, on the twenty-sixth, we reached Skardu and two days later flew to Rawalpindi. There we were taken into the home of friends, and gradually the immensity of our experience made itself felt. Dorky had come out to Pakistan to meet us and we stayed with Tahirah and Shahid Hamid and I'll never, never forget their kindness. Others stayed with Ata's family, and arrangements were quickly made for George to fly directly home for further hospital care. George, your toes had really done remarkably well, thanks to antibiotics and being dressed as gently and carefully as I could twice each day. Of course, your guts made a huge difference, but you certainly had some awful hours being carried over the rough paths.

BATES: Listening to the tapes with all of us together has made me think of things that were never entirely clear: For instance, what do you remember of the day of the accident, George?

BELL: First of all, I remember sitting up on the ridge in the wind for an eternity, belaying somebody (must have been Craig since Charlie and Bates were belaying Art), getting colder with every gust. Also, I could never get my windproof parka on over the down jacket since the arms had been cut too slim. This didn't help. Eventually Craig must have reached the end of the rope and untied for I recall then going up to Charlie and Bates to see how they were doing.

Just before the accident I had belayed Tony across the ice slope and Pete was preparing to lower Art, with the rest of you to pull. I thought the rope between Tony and me was fouled on Art or on the ropes across the slope to him, and that I had better hurry down the gully so as not to delay the lowering operation, or I might get pulled off. At the bottom of the gully it was necessary to start traversing the ice slope, and it appeared to me that a long step would take me to the first of some steps which Pete and Dee had cut across the slope. So I took the long step, the crampons didn't hold, and I was off.

I don't recall making any effort at all to stop; it seemed hopeless. I also felt I was falling many hundreds or thousands of feet. When I finally came to a stop I was hanging more or less freely in space and I assumed that the rope between Tony and me had snagged on a pinnacle and that perhaps we were not far from Camp VI. I am also pretty sure that I still had on my pack, mittens, and my glasses, but I couldn't see because they were packed with snow. Not wanting to spend the rest of my life—which seemed likely to be a very short time indeed— dangling at the end of the rope, the first priority was to try to get my weight off the rope by climbing the cliff. To that end I threw off my pack, thus losing glasses and mittens, which probably fell most of the way down the mountain—except for the small bag containing toilet kit, spare glasses, and expedition financial records, which lodged near Camp VI. Anyhow, I could then climb the cliff, which ended not far above me, and you know the rest.

CRAIG: If it hadn't been for the avalanche earlier, I would have been on the slope with you and been pulled down the mountain with you. About halfway down that wretched ice gully I had unroped so my rope could be used to lower Art down a bit further, and I was holding onto the rope which led to Art, and without any belay, when the avalanche came down over us. I certainly hung on for dear life. Then Dee roped me up and belayed me partway across the steep slope toward where Camp VII had been. I went on alone, but I had to rest about twenty minutes before my strength came back and I could work on the tent platform. I was almost all in. During that time, you all fell.

MOLENAAR: I remember, Bob, that after you came out from under that little avalanche I gave you a belay toward the site of Camp VII. You were really all in. Your crampons were coming off and you were having a helluva time getting them back on because they never really fitted those huge Mickey Mouse boots. I knew the avalanche had been a near thing and that you were nearly exhausted. When you were safely over the slope I went back to rejoin the party then working Art along the ice slope to a better place. I remember wandering about with all kinds of pitons and stuff hanging off my belt, stuff that Pete and I had gathered when we cleared the slopes above. It seemed like many hours that some of you had been sitting in the bitter wind up on the ridge belaying Art down. Pete and I had come down earlier and didn't fully realize how much was involved. After you unroped from me, Bob, I went back to lend a hand and tied onto Art's rope to Pete. Art had just been lowered over a small steep bit and we were getting ready to pendulum him over toward where we put up Camp VII. Tony was next to me while I took in the slack around my ax, driven into the ice. About 10 to 15 feet above us Charlie and Bob Bates were doing the same thing. I was looking up the slope at the time and suddenly saw George going down the ice on his back, feet first. I remember yelling, "Goddamn, there goes George!" A couple of seconds later everything else happened. I was quickly jerked off and slid on my stomach, face downward, so the slope was coming up at me. My only sensation was exhilaration, and thinking that I would be knocked out when I reached the rocks. Then suddenly I was brought to a stop a little way below the top of the rock. Another person was on top of me. It was Bob Bates. Charlie was about 25 feet below, lying among the rocks; Bell was starting to climb out of the ice gully and trying to protect his hands, because he had lost his gloves. Tony was a short distance above, on the lower part of the ice slope. Bob Bates then climbed down to Charlie and tied him to the end of a rope so I could belay him. He talked to Charlie, urging him to climb up to me. After Bell came up, Bates gave him some extra gloves, and we all traversed over to where Bob Craig was scraping out the ledge at VII. I didn't lose any gear in the fall; my pack was at VII, where I had dumped it a short time before.

HOUSTON: I have only the dimmest fragmented memories of that day. Bob, you've often described what happened when you painfully made your way down to where I was lying. What did you actually say and do?

BATES: Just what it says in the book, Charlie. You didn't know where you were and were very confused. We couldn't carry you or pull you up the rocks to Camp VII. At that point only you could do it—and fortunately you did!

HOUSTON: Well, I don't remember any of that. The rest of you were almost exhausted, I guess, and desperately trying to get some kind of shelter ready for all of us. It's lucky we were so close to the narrow ledge where we had put Camp VII some ten days earlier. Bob Craig was over there chopping out a platform, and I guess all of us tottered over to help put up tents, leaving Pete to anchor Art to the two ice axes. Does anyone have anything more to add to the taped description of that awful afternoon and night?

MOLENAAR: It certainly was a night to remember! You were in a nightmare of your own, Charlie. We worried about your being able to climb down, and also about George Bell. George had been frostbitten badly before, in South America, and besides he was a lot bigger than the rest of us; the blood had to travel a lot farther to reach his extremities and he was probably a lot more susceptible to frostbite. I remember that Craig and I had frostbitten heels and were hobbling on the balls of our feet. But George was in the worst shape and the condition of his feet was the main concern in our hurrying down to Base. I remember the trip from Camp VII back to Camp VI. I had a slightly cracked rib that made breathing a little difficult, and when I was in the tent at VII I had to lie on my back to breathe comfortably, half in and half out of the tent. It wasn't too bad a night, not too cold, and I was getting fresh air outside the tent. Next morning, after we started down, my leg began giving the most trouble. I finally found I had a cut about half an inch deep, but it didn't bleed because of the cold or the thickness of my blood at the altitude.

BATES: That morning we had trouble getting Charlie's crampons on and we didn't know how he would climb, but instinctively he climbed beautifully.

HOUSTON: I don't remember anything about the start. But I remember one terrible thing very clearly, all too clearly. Very soon after leaving Camp VII—I was leading down—I saw splotches of color on the rocks. They looked yellowish and it took a little time for me to realize that these were bloodstains where Art had fallen. For what seemed an eternity we had to climb down alongside these bloodstains, and fragments of the tent and the sleeping bag he had been wrapped in. No one mentioned this, and I guess I assumed that I was hallucinating. Anyway, I don't think we have ever discussed this until now. It was a terrible time.

MOLENAAR: Yes, we found the remains of Art's litter—a tangle of ropes along the track where the avalanche had taken him. The evidence was that Art had died almost immediately after the fall started. As a matter of fact, he was almost unconscious when we ourselves fell. When we got into VI, I recall getting into the ripped, snow-filled tents. For lack of anything to do, I got out my thread and needle and did a little sewing in the tent while the others were trying to get the snow out. That was a rough trip for Charlie.

BATES: As belay man coming down from Camp VII, I didn't want to be distracted by the stains. I focused my whole attention on belaying and watching where I put my feet. Nobody wanted to talk about what had happened. Charlie, do you remember that night at VI and how you kept waking up and putting your hands on cans of food and thinking you were in a warehouse? Next morning you seemed yourself and you did a great job of hacking away the ice so we could take the tent down. You were climbing well and seemed perfectly normal. George's feet were bad, though, and we were all worried about him.

BELL: I knew my feet were in bad shape, and we made no attempt to thaw them out since I still had a long way to walk to safety. Certainly no one in the party was strong enough to carry me! I had to get myself to Base. My hands were bad too, but after Bob Craig found the little bag with my glasses I was sure I could get down. Everybody was climbing safely, and the rope was a real spiritual bond between us.

BATES: Charlie, how much do you remember of the day we went from Camp VI to IV? You climbed well all day and you talked about George's feet, and frostbite that Bob and Dee seemed to have, too. You seemed mentally and physically completely normal except that you were slow. Do you remember how we worked together with George to chop out the good tent at VI? We were the last to get to Camp V, and at the top of the chimney we helped the others lower their loads and then we belayed them down. It was slow work and Pete kept calling to everybody to hurry. Your pack caught on a snag as we were lowering it, and when the others pulled from below and we pulled from above it slipped loose and clattered down off the mountain.

HOUSTON: I don't remember anything of the part from Camp VI to Camp V. But then my memory clears completely and I remember, just as vividly as if it were yesterday, standing at the top of House's Chimney. You know, we were always apprehensive, at least I was, about getting down in bad weather. It's not a terribly hard section but hard enough, and here we were, the weather not exactly good, all of us hurt and weak.

CRAIG: What I remember best about the trip from Camp VI to the chimney is how well everyone was doing. We were climbing carefully, slowly, but not too slowly, each one looking after the others. It was a good demonstration of how experience and guts can help. We were climbing almost instinctively, and that's what got us down.

HOUSTON: I don't remember who went down the chimney first. It doesn't matter, because each person went down so well.

But I do recall being determined to go last. I was the leader; I was responsible. I didn't feel at all handicapped even though my left eye was partly blind and I couldn't move my head very well. I must have made quite a scene by insisting that I go last.

BATES: After your load was lost, there wasn't much daylight left. I could see that if we took the time to lower my load, it would be dark before we could get down. I wanted to belay you down but you wanted to be last. There was no time to argue. Then it came to me that if I roped down quickly—for I was moving faster than you—and *carried my pack,* that would give you a little extra time before it got too dark to see at all; there was a low ceiling of storm clouds and the light was fading very fast. I remembered too from our Alaska days together that your vision in bad light is better than mine. The sudden idea seemed brilliant at the time but it didn't turn out that way. It was a serious mistake.

After I started down, you threw me a rope and insisted on my tying on. Then you held the rope and said that you had been the first one up the chimney and wanted to be the last one down. That was true but I was interested in speed, in our both getting down fast. When I got down the chimney I could still see fairly well, so I unroped and walked over to camp, where Tony asked me to help him guy the second tent, which he had been digging out. It didn't occur to me that you would have trouble in the chimney because you didn't have a pack and because Pete was holding a rope to you from below. It was only after Tony and I had been at the tent for five or ten minutes and heard Pete shouting that we realized you hadn't even started down yet. Then we did worry, plenty! Finally you did start and managed to get down nicely. It wasn't until this reunion that I realized how badly disoriented you were at the top of the chimney. Thank God you did all the right things.

SCHOENING: Well, I was off in the group to one side of the bottom of the chimney and I remember shouting to you to get started. It was getting dark and visibility was pretty bad when you finally did start, but once you began you came steadily and quite fast.

HOUSTON: After Bob left I remember, ever so clearly, thinking I couldn't possibly do it. There were three ropes in the chimney—one from 1938, one from 1939 (both hemp and too rotten to trust), and our good one. I couldn't tell them apart in the dark. I knew I couldn't use them but I would have to climb down, with Pete's rope from below keeping me from the big fall if I slipped. I thought, "I can't do it. I'll fall down on the others and knock them off. Better jump off to one side and get it over with." Well, it was a deeply emotional moment. I knelt in the snow and said the Lord's Prayer. Next thing I remember is being grasped by strong arms and helped into Camp IV.

BATES: You must have had a hideous time, a horrible experience, Charlie. It never occurred to me that you were mentally confused again, but I know nothing about head injuries and relapses. If you had done something crazy up there, I don't know how I could have stood it.

CRAIG: The rest of the descent was unremarkable, though I don't think anyone has commented on how we got down that overhanging tower just below Camp IV. That was always a tough one, but we made it, and down through the terribly deep soft snow to III, where we ate and rested for a long time before going on to II and our meeting with the porters.

STREATHER: As I have been listening to these tapes and thinking about the climb, I realize again how remarkable this party was. None of us were what one might call expert, at least by today's standards, and I was the least experienced of any. We had been through quite a bad ordeal, and we held together through a grueling descent. Without the strong bonds between us I don't believe we could have done it. There is quite a contrast between this descent and one or two of the famous tragedies, for instance Nanga Parbat in 1934. I imagine that some of the K2 experience helped get me through the Haramosh accident several years later. But I would rather not talk about that now. In our crisis we were physically and emotionally together.

BATES: Well, that's the story, and what more is there to say?

Perhaps that something from those storm-swept days has been fused into our bones and will never leave us. It has made a brotherhood, a special kind of friendship that is very rare and very precious.